Kanji	Meaning	Filipino
日	day, sun, Japan	araw
一	one	isa
国	country	bansa
人	person	mga tao
年	year	taon
大	large, big	Malaki
十	ten	sampu
二	two	dalawa
本	book, present, main, true, real	ito
中	in, inside, middle, mean, center	sa
長	long, leader	mahaba
出	exit, leave	Palabas
三	three	tatlo
時	time, hour	Oras
行	going, journey	Hilera
見	see, hopes, chances, idea, opinion, look at, visible	tingnan
月	month, moon	buwan
後	behind, back, later	Rear
前	in front, before	bago
五	five	Fives

All cards labeled N5.

Kanji	Meaning	Filipino
間	interval, space	sa pagitan
上	above, up	sa
東	east	silangan
四	four	apat
今	now	ngayon
金	gold	ginto
九	nine	siyam
入	enter, insert	ipasok
学	study, learning, science	pag-aaral
高	tall, high, expensive	matangkad
円	circle, yen, round	bilog
子	child, sign of the rat, 11PM-1AM	anak
外	outside	sa labas
八	eight	walo
六	six	anim
下	below, down, descend, give, low, inferior	sa ibaba
来	come, due, next, cause, become	darating
気	spirit, mind	espiritu
小	little, small	maliit
七	seven	pito

Kanji	Meaning	Filipino
山	mountain	bundok
話	tale, talk	kuwento
女	woman, female	babae
北	north	hilaga
午	noon, sign of the horse, 11AM-1PM	tanghali
百	hundred	daan
書	write	magsulat
先	before, ahead, previous, future, precedence	bago
名	name, noted, distinguished, reputation	pangalan
川	stream, river	ilog
千	thousand	libo
水	water	tubig
半	half, middle, odd number, semi-, part-half	kalahati
男	male	lalaki
西	west, Spain	kanluran
電	electricity	kuryente
校	exam, school, printing, proof, correction	pagsusulit
語	word, speech, language	pagsasalita
土	soil, earth, ground, Turkey	lupa
木	tree, wood	puno

All entries: N5

Kanji	Meaning	Filipino
聞 (N5)	hear, ask, listen	dinggin
食 (N5)	eat, food	kumain
車 (N5)	car	kotse
何 (N5)	what	Ano
南 (N5)	south	Timog
万 (N5)	ten thousand	sampung libo
毎 (N5)	every	bawat
白 (N5)	white	maputi
天 (N5)	heavens, sky, imperial	kalangitan
母 (N5)	mama, mother	ina
火 (N5)	fire	apoy
右 (N5)	right	tama
読 (N5)	read	basahin
友 (N5)	friend	kaibigan
左 (N5)	left	kaliwa
休 (N5)	rest, day off, retire, sleep	magretiro
父 (N5)	father	ama
雨 (N5)	rain	ulan
会 (N5)	meeting, meet, party, association, interview, join	partido
同 (N5)	same, agree, equal	sumang-ayon

Kanji	Meaning	Filipino
事 (N4)	matter, thing, fact, business, reason, possibly	katotohanan
自 (N4)	oneself	ang sarili
社 (N4)	company, firm, office, association, shrine	kumpanya
発 (N4)	discharge, departure, publish, emit, start from	paglabas
者 (N4)	someone, person	tao
地 (N4)	ground, earth	lupa
業 (N4)	business, vocation, arts, performance	negosyo
方 (N4)	direction, person, alternative	direksyon
新 (N4)	new	bago
場 (N4)	location, place	lokasyon
員 (N4)	employee, member, number, the one in charge	empleado
立 (N4)	stand up	tayo
開 (N4)	open, unfold, unseal	bukas
手 (N4)	hand	kamay
力 (N4)	power, strong, strain, bear up, exert	lakas
問 (N4)	question, ask, problem	magtanong
代 (N4)	substitute, change, convert, replace, period	henerasyon
明 (N4)	bright, light	Maliwanag
動 (N4)	move, motion, change, confusion, shift, shake	lumipat
京 (N4)	capital	Beijing

Kanji	Meaning	Filipino
目	eye, class, look, insight, experience, care, favor	Ulo
通	traffic, pass through, avenue, commute	sa pamamagitan ng
言	say	Pagsasalita
理	logic, arrangement, reason, justice, truth	Pangangatwiran
体	body, substance, object, reality, counter for images	katawan
田	rice field, rice paddy	bukid
主	lord, chief, master, main thing, principal	ang Panginoon
題	topic, subject	tanong
意	idea, mind, heart, taste, thought, desire	kahulugan
不	negative, non-, bad, ugly, clumsy	Huwag
作	make, production, prepare, build	Gumawa
用	utilize, business, service, use, employ	paggamit
度	degrees, occurrence, time, counter for occurrences	degree
強	strong	Malakas
公	public, prince, official, governmental	pampubliko
持	hold, have	hawakan
野	plains, field, rustic, civilian life	ligaw
以	by means of, because, in view of, compared with	Sa
思	think	isipin
家	house, home	Pamilya

Kanji	Meaning	Filipino
世 (N4)	generation, world, society, public	mundo
多 (N4)	many, frequent, much	marami
正 (N4)	correct, justice, righteous, 10**40	positibo
院 (N4)	Inst., institution, temple, mansion, school	ospital
心 (N4)	heart, mind, spirit	puso
界 (N4)	world	hangganan
教 (N4)	teach, faith, doctrine	turo
文 (N4)	sentence, literature, style, art, decoration	Teksto
元 (N4)	beginning, former time, origin	yuan
重 (N4)	heavy, heap up, pile up, nest of boxes, -fold	bigat
近 (N4)	near, early, akin, tantamount	malapit
考 (N4)	consider, think over	pagsusulit
画 (N4)	brush-stroke, picture	pagpipinta
海 (N4)	sea, ocean	dagat
売 (N4)	sell	ibenta
知 (N4)	know, wisdom	alam
道 (N4)	road-way, street, district, journey, course	Daan
集 (N4)	gather, meet, congregate, swarm, flock	magtipon
別 (N4)	separate, branch off, diverge, fork, another	magkahiwalay
物 (N4)	thing, object, matter	bagay

Kanji	Meaning	Tagalog
使	use	paggamit
品	goods, refinement, dignity, article	Produkto
計	plot, plan, scheme, measure	pamamaraan
死	death, die	patay
特	special	espesyal
私	private, I, me	pribado
始	commence, begin	simula
朝	morning, dynasty, regime, epoch, period	patungo
運	carry, luck, destiny, fate, lot, transport	Transport
終	end, finish	wakas
台	pedestal, a stand, counter for machines and vehicles	istasyon
広	wide, broad, spacious	malawak
住	dwell, reside, live, inhabit	tumira
真	true, reality, Buddhist sect	katotohanan
有	possess, have, exist, happen, occur, approx	taglay
口	mouth	bibig
少	few, little	mas kaunti
町	village, town, block, street	nayon
料	fee, materials	materyal
工	craft, construction	bapor

Kanji	Meaning	Tagalog
建 (N4)	build	magtayo
空 (N4)	empty, sky, void, vacant, vacuum	kalangitan
急 (N4)	hurry, emergency, sudden, steep	magmadali
止 (N4)	stop, halt	tumigil
送 (N4)	escort, send	escort
切 (N4)	cut, cutoff, be sharp	putulin
転 (N4)	revolve, turn around, change	umikot
研 (N4)	polish, study of, sharpen	pananaliksik
足 (N4)	leg, foot, be sufficient	paa
究 (N4)	research, study	Pag-aaral
楽 (N4)	music, comfort, ease	musika
起 (N4)	rouse, wake up, get up	gising na
着 (N4)	arrive, wear, counter for suits of clothing	dumating
店 (N4)	store, shop	mga tindahan
病 (N4)	ill, sick	may sakit
質 (N4)	substance, quality, matter, temperament	kalidad
待 (N4)	wait, depend on	Maghintay
試 (N4)	test, try, attempt, experiment, ordeal	pagsusulit
族 (N4)	tribe, family	Pamilya
銀 (N4)	silver	pilak

Kanji	Meaning	Filipino
早	early, fast	maaga
映	reflect, reflection, projection	Pagnilayan
親	parent, intimacy, relative, familiarity	magulang
験	verification, effect, testing	epekto
英	England, English	Ingles
医	doctor, medicine	medikal
仕	attend, doing, official, serve	opisyal
去	gone, past, quit, leave, elapse, eliminate, divorce	huminto
味	flavor, taste	panlasa
写	copy, be photographed, describe	kopya
字	character, letter, word, section of village	pagkatao
答	solution, answer	sagot
夜	night, evening	gabi
音	sound, noise	tunog
注	pour, irrigate, shed (tears), flow into	patubig
帰	homecoming, arrive at, lead to, result in	homecoming
古	old	sinaunang
歌	song, sing	awit
買	buy	bumili
悪	bad, vice, rascal, false, evil, wrong	masama

Kanji	Meaning	Tagalog
図	map, drawing, plan, unexpected, accidentally	mga mapa
週	week	linggo
室	room, apartment, chamber, greenhouse, cellar	silid
歩	walk, counter for steps	lakad
風	wind, air, style, manner	hangin
紙	paper	papel
黒	black	Itim
花	flower	bulaklak
春	springtime, spring (season)	tagsibol
赤	red	pula
青	blue, green	berde
館	building, mansion, large building, palace	gusali
屋	roof, house, shop, dealer, seller	bahay
色	color	kulay
走	run	tumakbo
秋	autumn	taglagas
夏	summer	tag-araw
習	learn	Pag-aaral
駅	station	istasyon
洋	ocean, western style	karagatan

All entries: N4

Kanji	Meaning	Filipino
旅 (N4)	trip, travel	paglalakbay
服 (N4)	clothing, admit, obey, discharge	mga damit
夕 (N4)	evening	gabi
借 (N4)	borrow, rent	humiram
曜 (N4)	weekday	Linggo
飲 (N4)	drink, smoke, take	uminom
肉 (N4)	meat	karne
貸 (N4)	lend	magpahiram
堂 (N4)	public chamber, hall	bulwagan
鳥 (N4)	bird, chicken	ibon
飯 (N4)	meal, boiled rice	bigas
勉 (N4)	exertion	bigay
冬 (N4)	winter	taglamig
昼 (N4)	daytime, noon	araw
茶 (N4)	tea	tsaa
牛 (N4)	cow	baka
魚 (N4)	fish	isda
兄 (N4)	elder brother, big brother	Kapatid
犬 (N4)	dog	aso
漢 (N4)	Sino-, China	Intsik

Kanji	Meaning	Filipino
政 (N3)	politics, government	Pamahalaan
議 (N3)	deliberation, consultation, debate, consideration	Pag-usapan
民 (N3)	people, nation, subjects	mga tao
連 (N3)	take along, lead, join, connect, party, gang, clique	sumali
対 (N3)	vis-a-vis, opposite, even, equal, versus, anti-	kabaligtaran
部 (N3)	section, bureau, dept, class, copy, part	seksyon
合 (N3)	fit, suit, join	suit
市 (N3)	market, city, town	lungsod
内 (N3)	inside, within, between, among, house, home	Sa loob
相 (N3)	inter-, mutual, together, each other	magkasama
定 (N3)	determine, fix, establish, decide	magtatag
回 (N3)	-times, round, game, revolve	umikot
選 (N3)	elect, select, choose, prefer	humalal
米 (N3)	rice, USA, metre	Meter
実 (N3)	reality, truth	katotohanan
関 (N3)	connection, barrier, gateway, involve, concerning	hadlang
決 (N3)	decide, fix, agree upon, appoint	Magpasya
全 (N3)	whole, entire, all, complete, fulfill	lahat
表 (N3)	surface, table, chart, diagram	lamesa
戦 (N3)	war, battle, match	labanan

Kanji	Meaning	Translation
経 (N3)	sutra, longitude, pass thru, expire, warp	mag-expire
最 (N3)	utmost, most, extreme	karamihan
現 (N3)	present, existing, actual	Kasalukuyan
調 (N3)	tune, tone, meter, key (music), writing style	Tune
化 (N3)	change, take the form of, influence, enchant	magbago
当 (N3)	hit, right, appropriate, himself	hit
約 (N3)	promise, approximately, shrink	humigit-kumulang
首 (N3)	neck	leeg
法 (N3)	method, law, rule, principle, model, system	batas
性 (N3)	sex, gender, nature	kasarian
要 (N3)	need, main point, essence, pivot, key to	kailangan
制 (N3)	system, law, rule	sistema
治 (N3)	reign, be at peace, calm down, subdue, quell	maghari
務 (N3)	task, duties	gawain
成 (N3)	turn into, become, get, grow, elapse, reach	maging
期 (N3)	period, time, date, term	tagal
取 (N3)	take, fetch, take up	sunduin
都 (N3)	metropolis, capital	kabisera
和 (N3)	harmony, Japanese style, peace, soften, Japan	pagkakasundo
機 (N3)	mechanism, opportunity, occasion, machine, airplane	makina

平 N3 even, flat, peace antas	**加** N3 add, addition, increase, join, include, Canada karagdagan	**受** N3 accept, undergo, answer (phone), take, get Tanggapin	**続** N3 continue, series, sequel magpatuloy
進 N3 advance, proceed, progress, promote advance	**数** N3 number, strength, fate, law, figures bilang	**記** N3 scribe, account, narrative tagasulat	**初** N3 first time, beginning maaga
指 N3 finger, point to, indicate, put into, play (chess) ipahiwatig	**権** N3 authority, power, rights awtoridad	**支** N3 branch, support, sustain suporta	**産** N3 products, bear, give birth, yield, childbirth Gumawa
点 N3 spot, point, mark, speck, decimal point punto	**報** N3 report, news, reward, retribution Mag-ulat	**済** N3 finish, come to an end, excusable, need not tapusin	**活** N3 lively, resuscitation, being helped, living masigla
原 N3 meadow, original, primitive, field, plain orihinal	**共** N3 together, both, neither, all, and, alike, with magkasama	**得** N3 gain, get, find, earn, acquire, can, may makakuha	**解** N3 unravel, notes, key, explanation solusyon

Kanji	Meaning	Tagalog
交 (N3)	mingle, mixing, association, coming & going	samahan
資 (N3)	assets, resources, capital, funds, data	mga mapagkukunan
予 (N3)	beforehand, previous, myself, I	nauna
向 (N3)	yonder, facing, beyond, confront, defy	lampas
際 (N3)	occasion, side, edge, verge, dangerous, adventurous	Okasyon
勝 (N3)	victory, win, prevail, excel	Manalo
面 (N3)	mask, face, features, surface	ibabaw
告 (N3)	revelation, tell, inform, announce	ipahayag
反 (N3)	anti-	kontra
判 (N3)	judgement, signature, stamp, seal	paghatol
認 (N3)	acknowledge, witness, discern, recognize	makilala
参 (N3)	nonplussed, three, going, coming, visiting	Makilahok
利 (N3)	profit, advantage, benefit	Kita
組 (N3)	association, braid, plait, construct, assemble	samahan
信 (N3)	faith, truth, fidelity, trust	pananampalataya
在 (N3)	exist, outskirts, suburbs, located in	umiiral
件 (N3)	affair, case, matter, item	pag-iibigan
側 (N3)	side, lean, oppose, regret	panig
任 (N3)	responsibility, duty, term, entrust to, appoint	responsibilidad
引 (N3)	pull, tug, jerk, admit, install, quote, refer to	hilahin

Kanji	Meaning	Tagalog
求	request, want, wish for, require, demand	kahilingan
所	place	lugar
次	next, order, sequence	pagkakasunod-sunod
昨	yesterday, previous	Kahapon
論	argument, discourse	pagtatalo
官	bureaucrat, the government	bureaucrat
増	increase, add, augment, gain, promote	tumaas
係	person in charge, connection, duty, concern oneself	tungkulin
感	emotion, feeling, sensation	damdamin
情	feelings, emotion, passion, sympathy	damdamin
投	throw, discard, abandon, launch into, join	itapon
示	show, indicate, point out, express, display	ipahiwatig
変	unusual, change, strange	kakaiba
打	strike, hit, knock, pound, dozen	welga
直	straightaway, honesty, frankness, fix, repair	katapatan
両	both, old Japanese coin, counter for vehicles, two	pareho
式	style, ceremony, rite, function, method, system	seremonya
確	assurance, firm, tight, hard, solid, confirm	katiyakan
果	fruit, reward, carry out, achieve, complete, end	prutas
容	contain, form, looks	naglalaman

Kanji	Meaning	Tagalog
必	invariably, certain, inevitable	hindi maiiwasan
演	performance, act, play, render, stage	pagganap
歳	year-end, age, occasion, opportunity	okasyon
争	contend, dispute, argue	alitan
談	discuss, talk	makipag-usap
能	ability, talent, skill, capacity	kasanayan
位	rank, grade, throne, crown, about, some	ranggo
置	placement, put, set, deposit, leave behind	paglalagay
流	current, a sink, flow, forfeit	kasalukuyang
格	status, rank, capacity, character	katayuan
疑	doubt, distrust, be suspicious, question	hinala
過	overdo, exceed, go beyond, error	lumampas
局	bureau, board, office, affair, conclusion	bureau
放	set free, release, fire, shoot, emit, banish	pagpapakawala
常	usual, ordinary, normal, regular	ordinaryong
状	status quo, conditions, circumstances, form	mga pangyayari
球	ball, sphere	bola
職	post, employment, work	Job
与	bestow, participate in, give, award, impart, provide	laban sa
供	submit, offer, present, serve (meal), accompany	ipasa

All entries: N3

Kanji	Meaning	Filipino
役 (N3)	duty, war, campaign, drafted labor, office, service	tungkulin
構 (N3)	posture, build, pretend	pustura
割 (N3)	proportion, comparatively, divide, cut, separate	proporsyon
費 (N3)	expense, cost, spend, consume, waste	gastos
付 (N3)	adhere, attach, refer to, append	sumunod
由 (N3)	wherefore, a reason	dahilan
説 (N3)	rumor, opinion, theory	tsismis
難 (N3)	difficult, impossible, trouble, accident, defect	mahirap
優 (N3)	tenderness, excel, surpass, actor, superiority	mahusay
夫 (N3)	husband, man	asawa
収 (N3)	income, obtain, reap, pay, supply, store	kita
断 (N3)	severance, decline, refuse, apologize	paghihiwalay
石 (N3)	stone	bato
違 (N3)	difference, differ	pagkakaiba
消 (N3)	extinguish, blow out, turn off, neutralize, cancel	pagkalagot
神 (N3)	gods, mind, soul	Diyos
番 (N3)	turn, number in a series	lumiko
規 (N3)	standard, measure	pamantayan
術 (N3)	art, technique, skill, means, trick, resources	Teknik
備 (N3)	equip, provision, preparation	Maghanda

宅 (N3) home, house, residence, our house, my husband Bahay	**害** (N3) harm, injury makakasama	**配** (N3) distribute, spouse, exile, rationing ipamahagi	**警** (N3) admonish, commandment magpayuhan
育 (N3) bring up, grow up, raise, rear itaas	**席** (N3) seat, mat, occasion, place upuan	**訪** (N3) call on, visit, look up, offer sympathy pagbisita	**乗** (N3) ride, power, multiplication, record Maramihang
残 (N3) remainder, leftover, balance tira	**想** (N3) concept, think, idea, thought konsepto	**声** (N3) voice tunog	**念** (N3) wish, sense, idea, thought, feeling, desire nais
助 (N3) help, rescue, assist tumulong	**労** (N3) labor, thank for, reward for, toil, trouble paggawa	**例** (N3) example, custom, usage, precedent halimbawa	**然** (N3) sort of thing, so, if so, in that case, well Syempre
限 (N3) limit, restrict, to best of ability limitasyon	**追** (N3) chase, drive away, follow, pursue, meanwhile habulin	**商** (N3) make a deal, selling, dealing in, merchant mangangalakal	**葉** (N3) leaf, plane, lobe, needle, blade, spear dahon

Kanji	Meaning	Translation
伝 (N3)	transmit, go along, walk along, follow, report	magpadala
働 (N3)	work, (kokuji)	Trabaho
形 (N3)	shape, form, style	form
景 (N3)	scenery, view	tanawin
好 (N3)	fond, pleasing, like something	nakalulugod
退 (N3)	retreat, withdraw, retire, resign, repel, expel	Umatras
頭 (N3)	head, counter for large animals	Ulo
負 (N3)	defeat, negative, -, minus, bear, owe	negatibo
渡 (N3)	transit, ford, ferry, cross, import, deliver	pagbibiyahe
失 (N3)	lose, error, fault, disadvantage, loss	Pagkawala
差 (N3)	distinction, difference, variation, discrepancy	pagkakaiba
末 (N3)	end, close, tip, powder, posterity	Tapusin
守 (N3)	guard, protect, defend, obey	Depensa
若 (N3)	young, if, perhaps, possibly, low number, immature	Bata
種 (N3)	species, kind, class, variety, seed	buto
美 (N3)	beauty, beautiful	Kagandahan
命 (N3)	fate, command, decree, destiny, life, appoint	buhay
福 (N3)	blessing, fortune, luck, wealth	pagpapala
望 (N3)	ambition, full moon, hope, desire, aspire to, expect	ambisyon
非 (N3)	un-, mistake, negative, injustice, non-	pagkakamali

Kanji	Meaning	Filipino
観	outlook, look, appearance, condition, view	hitsura
察	guess, presume, surmise, judge, understand	hulaan
段	grade, steps, stairs	Hakbang
横	sideways, side, horizontal, width, woof	panig
深	deep, heighten, intensify, strengthen	Malalim
申	have the honor to, sign of the monkey, 3-5PM	Unggoy
様	Esq., way, manner, situation, polite suffix	sitwasyon
財	property, money, wealth, assets	kayamanan
港	harbor	magkimkim
識	discriminating, know, write	diskriminasyon
呼	call, call out to, invite	mag-anyaya
達	accomplished, reach, arrive, attain	nagawa
良	good, pleasing, skilled	Mabuti
候	climate, season, weather	Panahon
程	extent, degree, law, formula, distance, limits	lawak
満	full, enough, pride, satisfy	Puno
敗	failure, defeat, reversal	Talunin
値	price, cost, value	halaga
光	ray, light	ray
路	path, route, road, distance	ruta

Kanji	Meaning	Translation
科 (N3)	department, course, section	kagawaran
積 (N3)	volume, product (x*y), acreage, contents, pile up	dami
他 (N3)	other, another, the others	iba pa
処 (N3)	dispose, manage, deal with, sentence, condemn	itapon
太 (N3)	plump, thick, big around	Makapal
客 (N3)	guest, visitor, customer, client	Bisita
否 (N3)	negate, no, noes, refuse, decline, deny	negate
師 (N3)	expert, teacher, master, army, war	dalubhasa
登 (N3)	ascend, climb up	pag-akyat
易 (N3)	easy, ready to, simple, fortune-telling, divination	Madali
速 (N3)	quick, fast	bilis
存 (N3)	suppose, be aware of, believe, feel	kunwari
飛 (N3)	fly, skip (pages), scatter	lumipad
殺 (N3)	kill, murder, butcher, slice off, split, diminish	pumatay
号 (N3)	nickname, number, item, title, pseudonym, name, call	palayaw
単 (N3)	simple, one, single, merely	simple
座 (N3)	squat, seat, cushion, gathering, sit	upuan
破 (N3)	rend, rip, tear, break, destroy, defeat, frustrate	nasira
除 (N3)	exclude, division (x, 3), remove, abolish, cancel	maliban
完 (N3)	perfect, completion, end	perpekto

Kanji	Meaning	Tagalog
降	descend, precipitate, fall, surrender	bumaba
責	blame, condemn, censure	sisihin
捕	catch, capture	mahuli
危	dangerous, fear, uneasy	Mapanganib
給	salary, wage, gift, allow, grant, bestow on	suweldo
苦	suffering, trial, worry, hardship, feel bitter	paghihirap
迎	welcome, meet, greet	maligayang pagdating
園	park, garden, yard, farm	hardin
具	tool, utensil, means, possess, ingredients	utensil
辞	resign, word, term, expression	Tumalikod
因	cause, factor, be associated with, depend on	dahil
馬	horse	kabayo
愛	love, affection, favourite	Pag-ibig
富	wealth, enrich, abundant	sagana
彼	he, that, the	siya
未	un-, not yet, hitherto, still, even now	hindi
舞	dance, flit, circle, wheel	sayaw
亡	deceased, the late, dying, perish	namatay
冷	cool, cold (beer, person), chill	ginaw
適	suitable, occasional, rare, qualified, capable	angkop

Kanji	Meaning	Filipino
婦 (N3)	lady, woman, wife, bride	babae
寄 (N3)	draw near, stop in, bring near, gather, collect	magpadala
込 (N3)	crowded, mixture, in bulk, included	masikip
顔 (N3)	face, expression	expression
類 (N3)	sort, kind, variety, class, genus	klase
余 (N3)	too much, myself, surplus, other, remainder	aking sarili
王 (N3)	king, rule, magnate	hari
返 (N3)	return, answer, fade, repay	bumalik
妻 (N3)	wife, spouse	asawa
背 (N3)	stature, height, back, behind, disobey, defy	tangkad
熱 (N3)	heat, temperature, fever, mania, passion	init
宿 (N3)	inn, lodging, relay station, dwell, lodge	bahay-panuluyan
薬 (N3)	medicine, chemical, enamel, gunpowder, benefit	gamot
頼 (N3)	trust, request	tiwala
覚 (N3)	memorize, learn, remember, awake, sober up	kabisaduhin
船 (N3)	ship, boat	ferry
途 (N3)	route, way, road	ruta
許 (N3)	permit, approve	aprubahan
抜 (N3)	slip out, extract, pull out, pilfer, quote, remove	kunin
便 (N3)	convenience	kaginhawaan

Kanji	Meaning	Tagalog
留	detain, fasten, halt, stop	pigilin
罪	guilt, sin, crime, fault, blame, offense	krimen
努	toil, diligent, as much as possible	masipag
精	refined, ghost, fairy, energy, vitality, semen	pinino
散	scatter, disperse, spend, squander	magkalat
静	quiet	Tahimik
婚	marriage	kasal
喜	rejoice, take pleasure in	magalak
浮	floating, float, rise to surface	lumutang
絶	discontinue, beyond, sever, cut off, abstain	itigil
幸	happiness, blessing, fortune	kaligayahan
押	push, stop, check, subdue, attach	itulak
倒	overthrow, fall, collapse, drop, break down	ibagsak
老	old man, old age, grow old	matanda
曲	bend, music, melody, composition	musika
払	pay, clear out, prune, banish, dispose of	magbayad
庭	courtyard, garden, yard	patyo
徒	junior, emptiness, vanity, futility, uselessness	junior
勤	diligence, become employed, serve	Sipag
遅	slow, late, back, later	mabagal

Kanji	Meaning	Translation
居 (N3)	reside, to be, exist, live with	tumira
雑 (N3)	miscellaneous	iba't-ibang
招 (N3)	beckon, invite, summon, engage	beckon
困 (N3)	quandary, become distressed, annoyed	inis
刻 (N3)	engrave, cut fine, chop, hash, mince, time, carving	naka-ukit
賛 (N3)	approve, praise, title or inscription on picture	aprubahan
抱 (N3)	embrace, hug, hold in arms	yakap
犯 (N3)	crime, sin, offense	krimen
恐 (N3)	fear, dread, awe	takot
息 (N3)	breath, respiration, son, interest (on money)	hininga
遠 (N3)	distant, far	malayong
戻 (N3)	re-, return, revert, resume, restore, go backwards	bumalik
願 (N3)	petition, request, vow, wish, hope	petisyon
絵 (N3)	picture, drawing, painting, sketch	larawan
越 (N3)	surpass, cross over, move to, exceed, Vietnam	malalampasan
欲 (N3)	longing, covetousness, greed, passion, desire	pagkahilig
痛 (N3)	pain, hurt, damage, bruise	sakit
笑 (N3)	laugh	tumawa
互 (N3)	mutually, reciprocally, together	kapwa
束 (N3)	bundle, sheaf, ream, tie in bundles, govern	bundle

Kanji	Meaning	Tagalog
似	becoming, resemble, counterfeit, imitate, suitable	kahawig
列	file, row, rank, tier, column	Hanay
探	grope, search, look for	Galugarin
逃	escape, flee, shirk, evade, set free	pagtakas
遊	play	paglilibot
迷	astray, be perplexed, in doubt, lost, err, illusion	naliligaw
夢	dream, vision, illusion	pangarap
君	old boy, name-suffix	matandang lalaki
閉	closed, shut	malapit
緒	thong, beginning, inception, end, cord, strap	simula
折	fold, break, fracture, bend, yield, submit	tiklop
草	grass, weeds, herbs, pasture, write, draft	damo
暮	livelihood, make a living, spend time	kabuhayan
酒	sake, alcohol	liqueur
悲	jail cell, grieve, sad, deplore, regret	malungkot
晴	clear up	malinaw
掛	hang, suspend, depend, arrive at, tax, pour	hang
到	arrival, proceed, reach, attain, result in	pagdating
寝	lie down, sleep, rest, bed, remain unsold	tulog
暗	darkness, disappear, shade, informal	kadiliman

盗 (N3) steal, rob, pilfer Magnanakaw	**吸** (N3) suck, imbibe, inhale, sip huminga	**陽** (N3) sunshine, yang principle, positive, male, heaven sikat ng araw	**御** (N3) honorable, manipulate, govern kagalang-galang
歯 (N3) tooth, cog ngipin	**忘** (N3) forget kalimutan	**雪** (N3) snow niyebe	**吹** (N3) blow, breathe, puff, emit, smoke suntok
娘 (N3) daughter, girl anak na babae	**誤** (N3) mistake, err, do wrong, mislead error	**洗** (N3) wash, inquire into, probe hugasan	**慣** (N3) accustomed, get used to, become experienced sanay na
礼 (N3) salute, bow, ceremony, thanks, remuneration seremonya	**窓** (N3) window, pane bintana	**昔** (N3) once upon a time, antiquity, old times antigong	**貧** (N3) poverty, poor kahirapan
怒 (N3) angry, be offended galit	**泳** (N3) swim paglangoy	**祖** (N3) ancestor, pioneer, founder Ang ninuno	**杯** (N3) counter for cupfuls, wine glass, glass, toast tasa

Kanji	Meaning	Tagalog
疲	exhausted, tire, weary	pagod
皆	all, everything	lahat
腹	abdomen, belly, stomach	tiyan
煙	smoke	usok
眠	sleep, die, sleepy	tulog
怖	dreadful, be frightened, fearful	malaking takot
耳	ear	tainga
頂	place on the head, receive, top of head, top, summit	tuktok
箱	box, chest, case, bin, railway car	kahon
晩	nightfall, night	gabi
寒	cold	malamig
髪	hair of the head	buhok
忙	busy, occupied, restless	abala
才	genius, years old, cubic shaku	henyo
靴	shoes	sapatos
恥	shame, dishonor	nakakahiya
偶	accidentally, even number, couple, man & wife	hindi sinasadya
偉	admirable, greatness, remarkable, conceited	kahanga-hanga
猫	cat	Cat
幾	how many, how much, how far, how long	ilan

党 N2 party, faction, clique partido	**協** N2 co-, cooperation kooperasyon	**総** N2 general, whole, all, full, total pangkalahatan	**区** N2 ward, district distrito
領 N2 jurisdiction, dominion, territory, fief, reign pangingibabaw	**県** N2 prefecture Prefecture	**設** N2 establishment, provision, prepare pagtatatag	**改** N2 reformation, change, modify, mend, renew repormasyon
府 N2 borough, urban prefecture, govt office Bahay	**査** N2 investigate mag-imbestiga	**委** N2 committee, entrust to, leave to, devote, discard komite	**軍** N2 army, force, troops, war, battle militar
団 N2 group, association pangkat	**各** N2 each, every, either bawat isa	**島** N2 island isla	**革** N2 leather, become serious, skin, hide, pelt katad
村 N2 town, village nayon	**勢** N2 forces, energy, military strength pwersa	**減** N2 dwindle, decrease, reduce, decline, curtail lumabo	**再** N2 again, twice, second time muli

Kanji	Meaning	Filipino
税 (N2)	tax, duty	buwis
営 (N2)	occupation, camp, perform, build, conduct (business)	trabaho
比 (N2)	compare, race, ratio, Philipines	ihambing
防 (N2)	ward off, defend, protect, resist	protektahan
補 (N2)	supplement, supply, make good, offset, compensate	suplemento
境 (N2)	boundary, border, region	hangganan
導 (N2)	guidance, leading, conduct, usher	patnubay
副 (N2)	vice-, duplicate, copy	Kopyahin
算 (N2)	calculate, divining, number, abacus, probability	kalkulahin
輸 (N2)	transport, send, be inferior	sasakyan
述 (N2)	mention, state, speak, relate	banggitin
線 (N2)	line, track	linya
農 (N2)	agriculture, farmers	agrikultura
州 (N2)	state, province	lalawigan
武 (N2)	warrior, military, chivalry, arms	mandirigma
象 (N2)	elephant, pattern after, imitate, image, shape	Elephant
域 (N2)	range, region, limits, stage, level	lugar
額 (N2)	forehead, tablet, plaque, framed picture, sum	noo
欧 (N2)	Europe	Europa
担 (N2)	shouldering, carry, raise, bear	palo

Kanji	Meaning	Tagalog
準 (N2)	semi-, correspond to, proportionate to, conform	umayon
賞 (N2)	prize, reward, praise	gantimpala
辺 (N2)	environs, boundary, border, vicinity	hangganan
造 (N2)	create, make, structure, physique	lumikha
被 (N2)	incur, cover, veil, brood over, shelter, wear	saklaw
技 (N2)	skill, art, craft, ability, feat, performance	Kasanayan
低 (N2)	lower, short, humble	mababa
復 (N2)	restore, return to, revert, resume	ibalik
移 (N2)	shift, move, change, drift, catch (cold, fire)	paglipat
個 (N2)	individual, counter for articles and military units	indibidwal
門 (N2)	gates	mga pintuan
課 (N2)	chapter, lesson, section, department, division	aralin
脳 (N2)	brain, memory	utak
極 (N2)	poles, settlement, conclusion, end	poste
含 (N2)	include, bear in mind, understand, cherish	isama
蔵 (N2)	storehouse, hide, own, have, possess	kamalig
量 (N2)	quantity, measure, weight, amount, consider	dami
型 (N2)	mould, type, model	hulma
況 (N2)	condition, situation	kondisyon
針 (N2)	needle, pin, staple, stinger	karayom

専 N2 specialty, exclusive, mainly, solely specialty	**谷** N2 valley Lambak	**史** N2 history, chronicle kasaysayan	**階** N2 storey, stair, counter for storeys of a building palapag
管 N2 pipe, tube, wind instrument, drunken talk tubo	**兵** N2 soldier, private, troops, army, warfare, strategy Kawal	**接** N2 touch, contact, adjoin, piece together hawakan	**細** N2 dainty, get thin, taper, slender, narrow masungit
効 N2 merit, efficacy, efficiency, benefit merito	**丸** N2 round, full, month, perfection, -ship, pills bilog	**湾** N2 gulf, bay, inlet Bay	**録** N2 record talaan
省 N2 focus, government ministry, conserve pokus	**橋** N2 bridge tulay	**岸** N2 beach baybayin	**周** N2 circumference, circuit, lap circumference
材 N2 lumber, log, timber, wood, talent tabla	**戸** N2 door pintuan	**央** N2 center, middle gitna	**券** N2 ticket tiket

Kanji	Meaning	Tagalog
編	compilation, knit, plait, braid, twist, editing	pagsasama-sama
捜	search, look for, locate	paghahanap
竹	bamboo	kawayan
並	row, and, besides, as well as, line up, rank with	Bukod sa
療	heal, cure	pagalingin
採	pick, take, fetch, take up	Pumili
森	forest, woods	kagubatan
競	emulate, compete with, bid, sell at auction	tularan
介	jammed in, shellfish, mediate, concern oneself with	shellfish
根	root, radical, head (pimple)	ugat
販	marketing, sell, trade	marketing
歴	curriculum, continuation, passage of time	kurikulum
将	leader, commander, general, admiral, or	pinuno
幅	hanging scroll, width	Lapad
般	carrier, carry, all	tagadala
貿	trade, exchange	kalakalan
講	lecture, club, association	panayam
林	grove, forest	kagubatan
装	attire, dress, pretend, disguise, profess	magbihis
諸	various, many, several, together	iba-iba

All entries: N2

劇 N2 drama, play drama	**河** N2 river Ilog	**航** N2 navigate, sail, cruise, fly mag-navigate	**鉄** N2 iron bakal
児 N2 newborn babe, child, young of animals Pediatric	**禁** N2 prohibition, ban, forbid pagbabawal	**印** N2 stamp, seal, mark, imprint, symbol, emblem Selyo	**逆** N2 inverted, reverse, opposite, wicked kabaligtaran
換 N2 interchange, period, charge, change? magbago	**久** N2 long time, old story matagal na panahon	**短** N2 short, brevity, fault, defect, weak point kalabisan	**油** N2 oil, fat langis
暴 N2 outburst, rave, fret, force, violence, cruelty Marahas	**輪** N2 wheel, ring, circle, link, loop gulong	**占** N2 fortune-telling, divining, forecasting, occupy manghuhula	**植** N2 plant halaman
清 N2 pure, purify, cleanse, exorcise, Manchu dynasty puro	**倍** N2 double, twice, times, fold doble	**均** N2 level, average antas	**億** N2 hundred million Bilyon

Kanji	Meaning	Filipino
圧	pressure, push, overwhelm, oppress, dominate	presyon
芸	technique, art, craft, performance, acting	pamamaraan
署	signature, govt office, police station	lagda
伸	expand, stretch, extend, lengthen, increase	Mabilis
停	halt, stopping	tumigil
爆	bomb, burst open, pop, split	pagputok
陸	land, six	lupain
玉	jewel, ball	hiyas
波	waves, billows, Poland	alon
帯	sash, belt, obi, zone, region	sash
延	prolong, stretching	tagal
羽	feathers, counter for birds, rabbits	balahibo
固	harden, set, clot, curdle	solid
則	rule, follow, based on, model after	panuntunan
乱	riot, war, disorder, disturb	kaguluhan
普	universal, wide(ly), generally, Prussia	pangkalahatan
測	fathom, plan, scheme, measure	pamamaraan
豊	bountiful, excellent, rich	mahusay
厚	thick, heavy, rich, kind, cordial, brazen, shameless	makapal
齢	age	edad

Kanji	Meaning	Filipino
囲 (N2)	surround, besiege, store, paling, enclosure	palibutan
卒 (N2)	graduate, soldier, private, die	nagtapos
略 (N2)	abbreviation, omission, outline, shorten, capture	pagdadaglat
承 (N2)	acquiesce, hear, listen to, be informed, receive	pagtanggap
順 (N2)	obey, order, turn, right, docility, occasion	sumunod
岩 (N2)	boulder, rock, cliff	bato
練 (N2)	practice, gloss, train, drill, polish, refine	pagsasanay
軽 (N2)	lightly, trifling, unimportant	gaan lang
了 (N2)	complete, finish	tapusin
庁 (N2)	government office	opisina ng pamahalaan
城 (N2)	castle	kastilyo
患 (N2)	afflicted, disease, suffer from, be ill	Naghihirap
層 (N2)	stratum, social class, layer, story, floor	layer
版 (N2)	printing block, printing plate, edition, impression	tatak
令 (N2)	orders, ancient laws, command, decree	utos
角 (N2)	angle, corner, square, horn, antlers	anggulo
絡 (N2)	entwine, coil around, get caught in	entwine
損 (N2)	damage, loss, disadvantage, hurt, injure	pagkasira
募 (N2)	recruit, campaign, gather (contributions)	bagong kasapi
裏 (N2)	back, amidst, in, reverse, inside, palm, sole	sa gitna

Kanji	Meaning	Translation
仏 (N2)	Buddha, the dead, France	Buddha
績 (N2)	exploits, unreeling cocoons	sinasamantala
築 (N2)	fabricate, build, construct	tela
貨 (N2)	freight, goods, property	kargamento
混 (N2)	mix, blend, confuse	timpla
昇 (N2)	rise up	Tumaas
池 (N2)	pond, cistern, pool, reservoir	Pool
血 (N2)	blood	dugo
温 (N2)	warm	mainit-init
季 (N2)	seasons	panahon
星 (N2)	star, spot, dot, mark	bituin
永 (N2)	eternity, long, lengthy	Magpakailanman
著 (N2)	renowned, publish, write, remarkable	kilalang tao
誌 (N2)	document, records	dokumento
庫 (N2)	warehouse, storehouse	bodega
刊 (N2)	publish, carve, engrave	mag-publish
像 (N2)	statue, picture, image, figure, portrait	imahe
香 (N2)	incense, smell, perfume	insenso
坂 (N2)	slope, incline, hill	libis
底 (N2)	bottom, sole, depth, bottom price, base, kind, sort	ibaba

Kanji	Meaning	Translation
布 (N2)	linen, cloth	tela
寺 (N2)	Buddhist temple	Templo
宇 (N2)	eaves, roof, house, heaven	bubong
巨 (N2)	gigantic, big, large, great	napakalaking
震 (N2)	quake, shake, tremble, quiver, shiver	nanginginig
希 (N2)	hope, beg, request, pray, beseech, Greece	pag-asa
触 (N2)	contact, touch, feel, hit, proclaim, announce	hawakan
依 (N2)	reliant, depend on, consequently, therefore, due to	ayon kay
籍 (N2)	enroll, domiciliary register, membership	magpalista
汚 (N2)	dirty, pollute, disgrace, rape, defile	marumi
枚 (N2)	sheet of..., counter for flat thin objects or sheets	mga sheet
複 (N2)	duplicate, double, compound, multiple	kumplikado
郵 (N2)	mail, stagecoach stop	mail
仲 (N2)	go-between, relationship	relasyon
栄 (N2)	flourish, prosperity, honor, glory, splendor	umunlad
札 (N2)	tag, paper money, counter for bonds, placard, bid	tag
板 (N2)	plank, board, plate, stage	plank
骨 (N2)	skeleton, bone, remains, frame	buto
傾 (N2)	lean, incline, tilt, trend, wane, sink, ruin, bias	ibuhos
届 (N2)	deliver, reach, arrive, report, notify, forward	naghahatid

Kanji	Meaning	Filipino
巻 (N2)	scroll, volume, book, part, roll up	Dami
燃 (N2)	burn, blaze, glow	Masunog
跡 (N2)	tracks, mark, print, impression	bakas
包 (N2)	wrap, pack up, cover, conceal	package
駐 (N2)	stop-over, reside in, resident	Station
弱 (N2)	weak, frail	mahina
紹 (N2)	introduce, inherit, help	ipakilala
雇 (N2)	employ, hire	upa
替 (N2)	exchange, spare, substitute, per-	palitan
預 (N2)	deposit, custody, leave with, entrust to	magdeposito
焼 (N2)	bake, burning	maghurno
簡 (N2)	simplicity, brevity	simple
章 (N2)	badge, chapter, composition, poem, design	badge
臓 (N2)	entrails, viscera, bowels	mga entrails
律 (N2)	rhythm, law, regulation, gauge, control	ritmo
贈 (N2)	presents, send, give to, award to, confer on	regalo
照 (N2)	illuminate, shine, compare, bashful	lumiwanag
薄 (N2)	dilute, thin, weak (tea)	payat
群 (N2)	flock, group, crowd, herd, swarm, cluster	pangkat
奥 (N2)	heart, interior	puso

Kanji	Meaning	Tagalog
詰	packed, close, pressed, reprove, rebuke, blame	pagalitan
双	pair, set, comparison, counter for pairs	doble
刺	thorn, pierce, stab, prick, sting, calling card	tinik
純	genuine, purity, innocence, net (profit)	puro
翌	the following, next	sa susunod
快	cheerful, pleasant, agreeable, comfortable	masayang
片	one-sided, leaf, sheet	dahon
敬	awe, respect, honor, revere	Magalang
悩	trouble, worry, in pain, distress, illness	gulo
泉	spring, fountain	tagsibol
皮	pelt, skin, hide, leather	balat
漁	fishing, fishery	pangingisda
荒	laid waste, rough, rude, wild	bastos
貯	savings, store, lay in, keep, wear mustache	matitipid
硬	stiff, hard	mahirap
埋	bury, be filled up, embedded	Bury
柱	pillar, post, cylinder, support	haligi
祭	ritual, offer prayers, celebrate, deify	ritwal
袋	sack, bag, pouch	bag
筆	writing brush, writing, painting brush, handwriting	pagpipinta ng brush

Kanji	Meaning	Tagalog
訓 (N2)	instruction, Japanese character reading	tagubilin
浴 (N2)	bathe, be favored with, bask in	maligo
童 (N2)	juvenile, child	anak
宝 (N2)	treasure, wealth, valuables	kayamanan
封 (N2)	seal, closing	selyo
胸 (N2)	bosom, breast, chest, heart, feelings	dibdib
砂 (N2)	sand	buhangin
塩 (N2)	salt	Asin
賢 (N2)	intelligent, wise, wisdom, cleverness	matalino
腕 (N2)	arm, ability, talent	pulso
兆 (N2)	portent, 10**12, trillion, sign, omen, symptoms	trilyon
床 (N2)	bed, floor, padding, tatami	kama
毛 (N2)	fur, hair, feather, down	buhok
緑 (N2)	green	berde
尊 (N2)	revered, valuable, precious, noble, exalted	mahalaga
祝 (N2)	celebrate, congratulate	magdiwang
柔 (N2)	tender, weakness, gentleness, softness	malambot
殿 (N2)	Mr., hall, mansion, palace, temple, lord	templo
濃 (N2)	concentrated, thick, dark, undiluted	puro
液 (N2)	fluid, liquid, juice, sap, secretion	likido

Kanji	Meaning	Tagalog
衣 (N2)	garment, clothes, dressing	mga damit
肩 (N2)	shoulder	balikat
零 (N2)	zero, spill, overflow, nothing, cipher	zero
幼 (N2)	infancy, childhood	pagkabata
荷 (N2)	baggage, shoulder-pole load	bagahe
泊 (N2)	overnight, put up at, ride at anchor, 3-day stay	magdamag
黄 (N2)	yellow	dilaw
甘 (N2)	sweet, coax, pamper, be content, sugary	matamis
臣 (N2)	retainer, subject	retainer
浅 (N2)	shallow, superficial, frivolous, wretched, shameful	mababaw
掃 (N2)	sweep, brush	magwalis
雲 (N2)	cloud	ulap
掘 (N2)	dig, delve, excavate	maghukay
捨 (N2)	discard, throw away, abandon, resign, reject	itapon
軟 (N2)	soft	malambot
沈 (N2)	sink, be submerged, subside, be depressed, aloes	lumubog
凍 (N2)	frozen, congeal, refrigerate	mag-freeze
乳 (N2)	milk, breasts	gatas
恋 (N2)	romance, in love, yearn for, miss, darling	pag-ibig
紅 (N2)	crimson, deep red	pula

Kanji	Meaning	Tagalog
郊 (N2)	outskirts, suburbs, rural area	Suburb
腰 (N2)	loins, hips, waist, low wainscoting	baywang
炭 (N2)	charcoal, coal	carbon
踊 (N2)	jump, dance, leap, skip	tumalon
冊 (N2)	tome, counter for books, volume	tome
勇 (N2)	courage, cheer up, be in high spirits, bravery	Matapang
械 (N2)	contraption, fetter, machine, instrument	instrumento
菜 (N2)	vegetable, side dish, greens	gulay
珍 (N2)	rare, curious, strange	mausisa
卵 (N2)	egg, ovum, spawn, roe	itlog
湖 (N2)	lake	lawa
喫 (N2)	consume, eat, drink, smoke, receive (a blow)	kumain
干 (N2)	dry, parch	tuyo
虫 (N2)	insect, bug, temper	insekto
刷 (N2)	printing, print	magsipilyo
湯 (N2)	hot water, bath, hot spring	mainit na tubig
溶 (N2)	melt, dissolve, thaw	Natunaw
鉱 (N2)	mineral, ore	mineral
涙 (N2)	tears, sympathy	luha
匹 (N2)	equal, head, counter for small animals	pantay

Kanji	Meaning	Tagalog
孫	grandchild, descendants	apo
鋭	pointed, sharpness, edge, weapon, sharp, violent	matalim
枝	bough, branch, twig, limb	sanga
塗	paint, plaster, daub, smear, coating	Pininturahan
軒	flats, counter for houses, eaves	flat
毒	poison, virus, venom, germ, harm, injury, spite	lason
叫	shout, exclaim, yell	sigaw
拝	worship, adore, pray to	pagsamba
氷	icicle, ice, hail, freeze, congeal	icicle
乾	drought, dry, dessicate, drink up, heaven, emperor	tagtuyot
棒	rod, stick, cane, pole, club, line	pamalo
祈	pray, wish	manalangin
拾	pick up, gather, find, go on foot, ten	magtipon
粉	flour, powder, dust	pulbos
糸	thread	sinulid
綿	cotton	bulak
汗	sweat, perspire	pawis
銅	copper	tanso
湿	damp, wet, moist	basa
瓶	flower pot, bottle, vial, jar, jug, vat, urn	bote

Kanji	Meaning	Tagalog
咲	blossom, bloom	mamulaklak
召	seduce, call, send for, wear, put on, ride in	pag-akitin
缶	tin can, container	palayok
隻	vessels, counter for ships, fish, birds, arrows	mga sasakyang-dagat
脂	fat, grease, tallow, lard, rosin, gum, tar	grasa
蒸	steam, heat, sultry, foment, get musty	singaw
肌	texture, skin, body, grain	kalamnan
耕	till, plow, cultivate	Pag-araro
鈍	dull, slow, foolish, blunt	mapurol
泥	mud, mire, adhere to, be attached to	putik
隅	corner, nook	sulok
灯	lamp, a light, light, counter for lights	lampara
辛	spicy, bitter, hot, acrid	maanghang
磨	grind, polish, scour, improve, brush (teeth)	giling
麦	barley, wheat	trigo
姓	surname	apelyido
筒	cylinder, pipe, tube, gun barrel, sleeve	silindro
鼻	nose, snout	ilong
粒	grains, drop, counter for tiny particles	butil
詞	part of speech, words, poetry	mga tula

Kanji	Meaning	Translation
胃 (N2)	stomach, paunch, crop, craw	tiyan
畳 (N2)	tatami mat, counter for tatami mats, fold	tiklop
机 (N2)	desk, table	desk
膚 (N2)	skin, body, grain, texture, disposition	balat
濯 (N2)	laundry, wash, pour on, rinse	labahan
塔 (N2)	pagoda, tower, steeple	tore
沸 (N2)	seethe, boil, ferment, uproar, breed	Pakuluan
灰 (N2)	ashes, puckery juice, cremate	abo
菓 (N2)	candy, cakes, fruit	kendi
帽 (N2)	cap, headgear	takip
枯 (N2)	wither, die, dry up, be seasoned	Nasaan
涼 (N2)	refreshing, nice and cool	nakakapreskong
舟 (N2)	boat, ship	bangka
貝 (N2)	shellfish	shellfish
符 (N2)	token, sign, mark, tally, charm	simbolo
憎 (N2)	hate, detest	Hate
皿 (N2)	dish, a helping, plate	Dish
肯 (N2)	agreement, consent, comply with	kasunduan
燥 (N2)	parch, dry up	tuyo
畜 (N2)	livestock, domestic fowl and animals	hayop

挟 N2 pinch, between kurutin	**曇** N2 cloudy weather, cloud up maulap	**滴** N2 drip, drop pagbagsak	**伺** N2 pay respects, visit, ask, inquire, question, implore nirerespeto
氏 N2 family name, surname, clan apelyido	**統** N2 overall, relationship, ruling, governing pangkalahatang	**保** N2 protect, guarantee, keep, preserve, sustain, support protektahan	**第** N2 No., residence tirahan
結 N2 tie, bind, contract, join, organize, do up hair kontrata	**派** N2 faction, group, party, clique, sect, school paksyon	**案** N2 plan, suggestion, draft, ponder, fear, proposition mungkahi	**策** N2 scheme, plan, policy, step, means Patakaran
基 N2 fundamentals, radical (chem), counter for machines mga panimula	**価** N2 value, price halaga	**提** N2 propose, take along, carry in hand magmungkahi	**挙** N2 raise, plan, project, behavior, actions itaas
応 N2 apply, answer, yes, OK, reply, accept mag-apply	**企** N2 undertake, scheme, design, attempt, plan isagawa	**検** N2 examination, investigate pagsusuri	**沢** N2 swamp swamp

裁 N1 tailor, judge, decision, cut out (pattern) sastre	**証** N1 evidence, proof, certificate sertipiko	**援** N1 abet, help, save tulong	**施** N1 alms, apply bandages, administer first-aid limos
井 N1 well, well crib, town, community mabuti	**護** N1 safeguard, protect Protektahan	**展** N1 unfold, expand magbuka	**態** N1 attitude, condition, figure, appearance saloobin
鮮 N1 fresh, vivid, clear, brilliant, Korea sariwa	**視** N1 inspection, regard as, see, look at inspeksyon	**条** N1 article, clause, item, stripe, streak artikulo	**幹** N1 tree trunk puno ng kahoy
独 N1 single, alone, spontaneously, Germany nag-iisa	**宮** N1 Shinto shrine, constellations, palace, princess konstelasyon	**率** N1 ratio, rate, proportion, %, coefficient, factor ratio	**衛** N1 defense, protection pagtatanggol
張 N1 lengthen, counter for bows & stringed instruments pahabain	**監** N1 oversee, official, govt office, rule, administer Mangasiwa	**環** N1 ring, circle, link, wheel bilog	**審** N1 hearing, judge, trial Pagsusuri

Kanji	Meaning	Translation
義 (N1)	righteousness, justice, morality, honor, loyalty	Katuwiran
訴 (N1)	accusation, sue, complain of pain, appeal to	Nagreklamo
株 (N1)	stocks, stump, shares, stock	tuod
姿 (N1)	figure, form, shape	pustura
閣 (N1)	tower, tall building, palace	tore
衆 (N1)	masses, great numbers, multitude, populace	masa
評 (N1)	evaluate, criticism, comment	suriin
影 (N1)	shadow, silhouette, phantom	Anino
松 (N1)	pine tree	puno ng pino
撃 (N1)	beat, attack, defeat, conquer	talunin
佐 (N1)	assistant, help	katulong
核 (N1)	nucleus, core, kernel	nuklear
整 (N1)	organize, arranging, tune, tone, meter, key (music)	ayusin
融 (N1)	dissolve, melt	matunaw
製 (N1)	made in..., manufacture	paggawa
票 (N1)	ballot, label, ticket, sign	balota
渉 (N1)	ford, ferry, port	ferry
響 (N1)	echo, also N5116, sound, resound, ring, vibrate	sigaw
推 (N1)	conjecture, infer, guess, suppose, support	haka-haka
請 (N1)	solicit, invite, ask	pakiusap

Kanji	Meaning	Filipino
器 (N1)	utensil, vessel, receptacle, implement, instrument	utensil
士 (N1)	gentleman, samurai	ginoo
討 (N1)	chastise, attack, defeat, destroy, conquer	pagbutihin
攻 (N1)	aggression, attack	pag-atake
崎 (N1)	promontory, cape, spit	promontory
督 (N1)	coach, command, urge, lead, supervise	coach
授 (N1)	impart, instruct, grant, confer	Ibigay
催 (N1)	sponsor, hold (a meeting), give (a dinner)	sponsor
及 (N1)	reach out, exert, exercise, cause	magsikap
憲 (N1)	constitution, law	konstitusyon
摘 (N1)	pinch, pick, pluck, trim, clip, summarize	Pumili
系 (N1)	lineage, system	angkan
批 (N1)	criticism, strike	pagpuna
郎 (N1)	son, counter for sons	anak
健 (N1)	healthy, health, strength, persistence	Malusog
盟 (N1)	alliance, oath	alyansa
従 (N1)	accompany, obey, submit to, comply, follow	samahan
修 (N1)	discipline, conduct oneself well, study, master	disiplina
隊 (N1)	regiment, party, company, squad	pamumula
織 (N1)	weave, fabric	Weave

Kanji	Meaning	Tagalog
拡 (N1)	broaden, extend, expand, enlarge	palawakin
故 (N1)	happenstance, especially	pangyayari
振 (N1)	shake, wave, wag, swing	umiling
弁 (N1)	valve, petal, braid, speech, dialect, discrimination	balbula
就 (N1)	concerning, settle, take position, depart	tungkol sa
異 (N1)	uncommon, queerness, strangeness, wonderful	bihira
献 (N1)	offering, counter for drinks, present, offer	alok
厳 (N1)	stern, strictness, severity, rigidity	istrikto
維 (N1)	fiber, tie, rope	hibla
浜 (N1)	seacoast, beach, seashore	beach
遺 (N1)	bequeath, leave behind, reserve	bequeath
塁 (N1)	bases, fort, rampart, walls, base(ball)	mga batayan
邦 (N1)	home country, country, Japan	bansa
素 (N1)	elementary, principle, naked, uncovered	elementarya
遣 (N1)	despatch, send, give, donate, do, undertake	humahamak
抗 (N1)	confront, resist, defy, oppose	humarap
模 (N1)	imitation, copy, mock	panggagaya
雄 (N1)	masculine, male, hero, leader, superiority	panlalaki
益 (N1)	benefit, gain, profit, advantage	kapaki-pakinabang
緊 (N1)	tense, solid, hard, reliable, tight	masikip

Kanji	Meaning	Filipino
標 (N1)	signpost, seal, mark, stamp, imprint	selyo
宣 (N1)	proclaim, say, announce	magpahayag
昭 (N1)	shining, bright	maliwanag
廃 (N1)	abolish, obsolete, cessation, discarding, abandon	ipawalang-bisa
伊 (N1)	Italy, that one	Italya
江 (N1)	creek, inlet, bay	sapa
僚 (N1)	colleague, official, companion	kasamahan
吉 (N1)	good luck, joy, congratulations	pagbati
皇 (N1)	emperor	Emperor
臨 (N1)	look to, face, meet, confront, attend, call on	mukha
踏 (N1)	step, trample, carry through, appraise	pagyurak
壊 (N1)	demolition, break, destroy	demolisyon
債 (N1)	bond, loan, debt	utang
興 (N1)	entertain, revive, retrieve, interest, pleasure	aliw
源 (N1)	source, origin	pinagmulan
儀 (N1)	ceremony, rule, affair, case, a matter	seremonya
創 (N1)	genesis, wound, injury, hurt, start, originate	genesis
障 (N1)	hinder, hurt, harm	hadlangan
継 (N1)	inherit, succeed, patch, graft (tree)	magmana
筋 (N1)	muscle, sinew, tendon, fiber, plot, plan, descent	kalamnan

Kanji	Meaning	Tagalog
闘 (N1)	fight, war	lumaban
葬 (N1)	interment, bury, shelve	panghihimasok
避 (N1)	evade, avoid, avert, ward off, shirk, shun	iwasan
司 (N1)	director, official, govt office, rule, administer	direktor
康 (N1)	ease, peace	kadalian
善 (N1)	virtuous, good, goodness	mabuti
逮 (N1)	apprehend, chase	mahuli
迫 (N1)	urge, force, imminent, spur on	lakas
惑 (N1)	beguile, delusion, perplexity	maling akala
崩 (N1)	crumble, die, demolish, level	gumuho
紀 (N1)	chronicle, account, narrative, history, annals	salaysay
聴 (N1)	listen, headstrong, naughty, careful inquiry	pakinggan
脱 (N1)	undress, removing, escape from, get rid of	naghubad
級 (N1)	class, rank, grade	antas
博 (N1)	Dr., command, esteem, win acclaim, Ph.D.,	pagpapahalaga
締 (N1)	tighten, tie, shut, lock, fasten	higpitan
救 (N1)	salvation, save, help, rescue, reclaim	makatipid
執 (N1)	tenacious, take hold, grasp, take to heart	mabait
房 (N1)	tassel, tuft, fringe, bunch, lock (hair)	palawit
撤 (N1)	remove, withdraw, disarm, dismantle, reject, exclude	bawiin

Kanji	Meaning	Tagalog
削 (N1)	plane, sharpen, whittle, pare	patalasin
密 (N1)	secrecy, density (pop), minuteness, carefulness	lihim
措 (N1)	set aside, give up, suspend, discontinue, lay aside	suspindihin
志 (N1)	intention, plan, resolve, aspire, motive, hopes	balak
載 (N1)	ride, board, get on, place, spread, 10**44	sumakay
陣 (N1)	camp, battle array, ranks, position	kampo
我 (N1)	ego, I, selfish, our, oneself	ego
為 (N1)	do, change, make, benefit	benepisyo
抑 (N1)	repress, well, now, in the first place, push	panunumbat
幕 (N1)	curtain, bunting, act of play	kurtina
染 (N1)	dye, color, paint, stain, print	pangulay
奈 (N1)	Nara, what?	Ano
傷 (N1)	wound, hurt, injure, impair, pain, injury, cut	nasasaktan
択 (N1)	choose, select, elect, prefer	pumili
秀 (N1)	excel, excellence, beauty, surpass	kahusayan
徴 (N1)	indications, sign, omen, symptom, collect, seek	mga indikasyon
弾 (N1)	bullet, twang, flip, snap	bala
償 (N1)	reparation, make up for, recompense, redeem	pagpapahiya
功 (N1)	achievement, merits, success, honor, credit	nakamit
拠 (N1)	foothold, based on, follow, therefore	bukana

Kanji	Meaning	Tagalog
秘	secret, conceal	lihim
拒	repel, refuse, reject, decline	Tumanggi
刑	punish, penalty, sentence, punishment	parusa
塚	hillock, mound	tambak
致	doth, do, send, forward, cause, exert, incur, engage	pasulong
繰	winding, reel, spin, turn (pages), look up, refer to	reel
尾	tail, end, counter for fish, lower slope of mountain	buntot
描	sketch, compose, write, draw, paint	sketch
鈴	small bell, buzzer	kampana
盤	tray, shallow bowl, platter, tub, board	tray
項	paragraph, nape of neck, clause, item	talata
喪	miss, mourning	pagdadalamhati
伴	consort, accompany, bring with, companion	Kasosyo
養	foster, bring up, rear, develop, nurture	tagapagtaguyod
懸	suspend, hang, 10%, install, depend, consult	suspindihin
街	boulevard, street, town	kalye
契	pledge, promise, vow	pangako
掲	put up (a notice), put up, hoist, display	hoist
躍	leap, dance, skip	tumalon
棄	abandon, throw away, discard, resign, reject	inabandona

Kanji	Meaning	Tagalog
邸	residence, mansion	tirahan
縮	shrink, contract, shrivel, wrinkle, reduce	Paliitin
還	send back, return	bumalik
属	belong, genus, subordinate official, affiliated	nabibilang
慮	prudence, thought, concern, consider, deliberate	isaalang-alang
枠	frame, framework, spindle, spool	balangkas
恵	favor, blessing, grace, kindness	pabor
露	dew, tears, expose, Russia	hamog
節	clause, stanza, honor, joint, knuckle, knob, knot	tagal
需	demand, request, need	hinihingi
射	shoot, shine into, onto, archery	Shoot
購	subscription, buy	pagbili
揮	brandish, wave, wag, swing, shake	Wave
充	allot, fill	maglagay
貢	tribute, support, finance	pagkilala
鹿	deer	usa
却	instead, on the contrary, rather	ngunit
端	edge, origin, end, point, border, verge, cape	wakas
賃	fare, fee, hire, rent, wages, charge	upa
獲	seize, get, find, earn, acquire, can, may, able to	Makakuha

郡 N1 county, district county	**併** N1 join, get together, unite, collective sumali	**徹** N1 penetrate, clear, pierce, strike home tumagos	**貴** N1 precious, value, prize, esteem, honor mahalaga
衝 N1 collide, brunt, highway, opposition (astronomy) bumangga	**焦** N1 char, hurry, impatient, irritate, burn, scorch magmadali	**奪** N1 rob, take by force, snatch away, dispossess, plunder ninakawan	**災** N1 disaster, calamity, woe, curse, evil kalamidad
浦 N1 bay, creek, inlet, gulf, beach, seacoast bay	**析** N1 chop, divide, tear, analyze tumaga	**譲** N1 defer, turnover, transfer, convey turnover	**称** N1 appellation, praise, admire, name, title, fame apela
納 N1 settlement, obtain, reap, pay, supply, store pag-areglo	**樹** N1 timber trees, wood kahoy	**挑** N1 challenge, contend for, make love to hamon	**誘** N1 entice, lead, tempt, invite, ask, call for mang-akit
紛 N1 distract, be mistaken for, go astray, divert makagambala	**至** N1 climax, arrive, proceed, reach, attain, result in kasukdulan	**宗** N1 religion, sect, denomination, main point, origin relihiyon	**促** N1 stimulate, urge, press, demand, incite pasiglahin

Kanji	Meanings	Tagalog
慎 (N1)	humility, be careful, discrete, prudent	pagpapakumbaba
控 (N1)	withdraw, draw in, hold back, refrain from	bawiin
智 (N1)	wisdom, intellect, reason	karunungan
握 (N1)	grip, hold, mould sushi, bribe	pagkakahawak
宙 (N1)	mid-air, air, space, sky, memorization	sansinukob
俊 (N1)	sagacious, genius, excellence	malandi
銭 (N1)	coin, .01 yen, money	pera
渋 (N1)	astringent, hesitate, reluctant, have diarrhea	mag-atubiling
銃 (N1)	gun, arms	pistol
操 (N1)	maneuver, manipulate, operate, steer, chastity	pagmamanipula
携 (N1)	portable, carry (in hand), armed with, bring along	magdala
診 (N1)	checkup, seeing, diagnose, examine	pag-checkup
託 (N1)	consign, requesting, entrusting with, pretend, hint	magbigay
撮 (N1)	snapshot, take pictures	snapshot
誕 (N1)	nativity, be born, declension, lie, be arbitrary	pagkatao
侵 (N1)	encroach, invade, raid, trespass, violate	encroach
括 (N1)	fasten, tie up, arrest, constrict	i-fasten
謝 (N1)	apologize, thank, refuse	humingi ng tawad
駆 (N1)	drive, run, gallop, advance, inspire, impel	magmaneho
透 (N1)	transparent, permeate, filter, penetrate	transparent

津 N1 haven, port, harbor, ferry magkimkim	**壁** N1 wall, lining (stomach), fence pader	**稲** N1 rice plant halaman ng bigas	**仮** N1 sham, temporary, interim, assumed (name), informal pansamantala
裂 N1 split, rend, tear basag	**敏** N1 cleverness, agile, alert katalinuhan	**是** N1 just so, this, right, justice hustisya	**排** N1 repudiate, exclude, expel, reject tumanggi
裕 N1 abundant, rich, fertile sagana	**堅** N1 strict, hard, solid, tough, tight, reliable mahigpit	**訳** N1 translate, reason, circumstance, case Isalin	**芝** N1 turf, lawn damuhan
綱 N1 hawser, class (genus), rope, cord, cable lubid	**典** N1 code, ceremony, law, rule Code	**賀** N1 congratulations, joy Batiin	**扱** N1 handle, entertain, thresh, strip hawakan
顧 N1 look back, review, examine oneself, turn around pagsusuri	**弘** N1 vast, broad, wide malawak	**看** N1 watch over, see tingnan	**訟** N1 sue, accuse akusahan

Kanji	Meaning	Filipino
戒	commandment	utos
祉	welfare, happiness	kapakanan
誉	reputation, praise, honor, glory	reputasyon
歓	delight, joy	galak
奏	play music, speak to a ruler, complete	Maglaro
勧	persuade, recommend, advise, encourage, offer	hikayatin
騒	boisterous, make noise, clamor, disturb, excite	Kaguluhan
閥	clique, lineage, pedigree, faction, clan	pangkatin
甲	armor, high (voice), A grade, first class, former	nakasuot ng sandata
縄	straw rope, cord	kurdon
郷	home town, village, native place, district	nayon
揺	swing, shake, sway, rock, tremble, vibrate	ugoy
免	excuse, dismissal	pasensya
既	previously, already, long ago	dati
薦	recommend, mat, advise, encourage, offer	inirerekumenda
隣	neighboring	kalapit
華	splendor, flower, petal, shine, luster, ostentatious	kamahalan
範	pattern, example, model	pattern
隠	conceal, hide, cover	itago
徳	benevolence, virtue, goodness, commanding respect	kabutihan

Kanji	Meaning	Tagalog
哲	philosophy, clear	pilosopiya
杉	cedar, cryptomeria	Cedar
釈	explanation	paliwanag
己	self, snake, serpent	ahas
妥	gentle, peace, depravity	banayad
威	intimidate, dignity, majesty, menace, threaten	Prestige
豪	overpowering, great, powerful, excelling, Australia	sobrang lakas
熊	bear	Bear
滞	stagnate, be delayed, overdue, arrears	Pagwawalang-kilos
微	delicate, minuteness, insignificance	maselan
隆	hump, high, noble, prosperity	umbok
症	symptoms, illness	sintomas
暫	temporarily, a while, moment, long time	pansamantalang
忠	loyalty, fidelity, faithfulness	Matapat
倉	godown, warehouse, storehouse, cellar, treasury	bodega
彦	lad, boy (ancient)	batang lalaki
肝	liver, pluck, nerve, chutzpah	atay
喚	yell, cry, scream	sigaw
沿	run alongside, follow along, run along, lie along	kasama
妙	exquisite, strange, queer, mystery, miracle	kahanga-hanga

Kanji	Meaning	Tagalog
唱	chant, recite, call upon, yell	umawit
阿	Africa, flatter, fawn upon, corner, nook, recess	Africa
索	cord, rope	lubid
誠	sincerity, admonish, warn, prohibit, truth	katapatan
襲	attack, advance on, succeed to, pile, heap	pag-atake
懇	sociable, kind, courteous, hospitable, cordial	palakaibigan
俳	haiku, actor	aktor
柄	design, pattern, build, nature, handle, crank	disenyo
驚	wonder, be surprised, frightened, amazed	magtaka
麻	hemp, flax	abaka
李	plum	plum
浩	wide expanse, abundance, vigorous	kasaganaan
剤	dose, medicine, drug	gamot
瀬	rapids, current, torrent, shallows, shoal	kasalukuyang
趣	gist, proceed to, tend, become	maging
陥	collapse, fall into, cave in, fall (castle)	pagbagsak
斎	purification, Buddhist food, room, worship, avoid	paglilinis
貫	pierce, 8 1, 3lbs, penetrate, brace	tumusok
仙	hermit, wizard, cent	ermitanyo
慰	consolation, amusement, seduce, cheer, console	ginhawa

Kanji	Meaning	Tagalog
序	preface, beginning, order, precedence, occasion	paunang salita
兼	concurrently, and	kasabay
聖	holy, saint, sage, master, priest	Banal
旨	delicious, relish, show a liking for, purport, will	masarap
即	instant, namely, as is, conform, agree, adapt	instant
柳	willow	willow
舎	cottage, inn, hut, house, mansion	kubo
偽	falsehood, lie, deceive, pretend, counterfeit	kasinungalingan
較	contrast, compare	Paghambingin
覇	hegemony, supremacy, leadership, champion	hegemony
詳	detailed, full, minute, accurate, well-informed	detalyado
抵	resist, reach, touch	lumaban
脅	threaten, coerce	Nagbabanta
茂	overgrown, grow thick, be luxuriant	napuno
犠	sacrifice	sakripisyo
旗	national flag, banner, standard	bandila
距	long-distance	distansya
雅	gracious, elegant, graceful, refined	matikas
飾	decorate, ornament, adorn, embellish	Palamutihan
網	netting, network	network

Kanji	Meaning	Translation
竜 (N1)	dragon, imperial	Dragon
詩 (N1)	poem, poetry	mga tula
繁 (N1)	luxuriant, thick, overgrown, frequency, complexity	Magulo
翼 (N1)	wing, plane, flank	pakpak
潟 (N1)	lagoon	laguna
敵 (N1)	enemy, foe, opponent	kalaban
魅 (N1)	fascination, charm, bewitch	Charm
嫌 (N1)	dislike, detest, hate	Hinala
斉 (N1)	adjusted, alike, equal, similar variety of	nababagay
敷 (N1)	spread, pave, sit, promulgate	kumalat
擁 (N1)	hug, embrace, possess, protect, lead	yakap
圏 (N1)	sphere, circle, radius, range	globo
酸 (N1)	acid, bitterness, sour, tart	acid
罰 (N1)	penalty, punishment	Parusahan
滅 (N1)	destroy, ruin, overthrow, perish	sirain
礎 (N1)	cornerstone, foundation stone	pundasyon
腐 (N1)	rot, decay, sour	Rot
潮 (N1)	tide, salt water, opportunity	pag-ulan
梅 (N1)	plum	plum
尽 (N1)	exhaust, use up, run out of, befriend, serve	Exhaust

Kanji	Meaning	Filipino
僕 (N1)	me, I (male)	ako
桜 (N1)	cherry	seresa
滑 (N1)	slippery, slide, slip, flunk	madulas
孤 (N1)	orphan, alone	ulila
炎 (N1)	inflammation, flame, blaze	pamamaga
賠 (N1)	compensation, indemnify	kabayaran
句 (N1)	phrase, clause, sentence, passage, paragraph	parirala
鋼 (N1)	steel	bakal
頑 (N1)	stubborn, foolish, firmly	matigas ang ulo
鎖 (N1)	chain, irons, connection	kadena
彩 (N1)	coloring, paint, makeup	pangkulay
摩 (N1)	chafe, rub, polish, grind, scrape	polish
励 (N1)	encourage, be diligent, inspire	Hikayatin
縦 (N1)	vertical, length, height, self-indulgent, wayward	patayo
輝 (N1)	radiance, shine, sparkle, gleam, twinkle	Napakatalino
蓄 (N1)	amass, keeping a concubine, phonograph	ponograpiya
軸 (N1)	axis, pivot, stem, stalk, counter for book scrolls	aksis
巡 (N1)	patrol, go around, circumference	patrol
稼 (N1)	earnings, work, earn money	kita
瞬 (N1)	wink, blink, twinkle	kumindat

Kanji	Meaning	Tagalog
砲 (N1)	cannon, gun	baril
噴 (N1)	erupt, spout, emit, flush out	wisik
誇 (N1)	boast, be proud, pride, triumphantly	magyabang
祥 (N1)	auspicious, happiness, good omen	Nakakatawa
牲 (N1)	animal sacrifice, offering	Sakripisyo
秩 (N1)	regularity, salary, order	suweldo
帝 (N1)	sovereign, the emperor, god, creator	emperor
宏 (N1)	wide, large	malawak
唆 (N1)	tempt, seduce, instigate, promote	tuksuhin
阻 (N1)	thwart, separate from, prevent, obstruct, deter	pigilan
泰 (N1)	peaceful, calm, peace, easy, Thailand	mapayapa
賄 (N1)	bribe, board, supply, finance	suhol
撲 (N1)	slap, strike, hit, beat, tell, speak	sampal
堀 (N1)	ditch, moat, canal	kanal
菊 (N1)	chrysanthemum	krisantemo
絞 (N1)	strangle, constrict, wring	masungit
縁 (N1)	affinity, relation, connection, edge, border	pagkakaugnay
唯 (N1)	solely, only, merely, simply	lamang
膨 (N1)	swell, get fat, thick	Mag-swell
矢 (N1)	dart, arrow	dart

Kanji	Meaning	Tagalog
耐	-proof, enduring	pagbabata
塾	cram school, private school	Pribadong paaralan
漏	leak, escape, time	tumagas
慶	jubilation, congratulate, rejoice, be happy	Ipagdiwang
猛	fierce, rave, rush, become furious, wildness	mabangis
芳	perfume, balmy, flavorable, fragrant	pabango
懲	penal, chastise, punish, discipline	penal
剣	sabre, sword, blade, clock hand	Tabak
彰	patent, clear	patent
棋	chess piece, Japanese chess, shogi	chess
丁	street, ward, town	kalye
恒	constancy, always	Patuloy
揚	hoist, fry in deep fat	hoist
冒	risk, face, defy, dare, damage, assume (a name)	Panganib
之	of, this	ito
倫	ethics, companion	kasama
陳	exhibit, state, relate, explain	nagpapakita
憶	recollection, think, remember	Magugunita
梨	pear tree	peras
仁	humanity, virtue, benevolence, charity, man, kernel	kabutihan

All kanji marked N1.

Kanji	Meanings	Filipino
克	overcome, kindly, skillfully	pagtagumpayan
岳	point, peak, mountain	punto
概	outline, condition, approximation, generally	balangkas
拘	arrest, seize, concerned, adhere to, despite	pagdakip
墓	grave, tomb	libingan
黙	silence, become silent, stop speaking, leave as is	katahimikan
須	ought, by all means, necessarily	kinakailangan
偏	partial, side, left-side radical, inclining, biased	Bahagyang
雰	atmosphere, fog	kapaligiran
遇	interview, treat, entertain, receive, deal with	pakikipanayam
諮	consult with	Kumonsulta
狭	cramped, narrow, contract, tight	makitid
卓	eminent, table, desk, high	tanyag
亀	tortoise, turtle	pagong
糧	provisions, food, bread	butil
簿	register, record book	magparehistro
炉	hearth, furnace, kiln, reactor	hurno
牧	breed, care for, shepherd, feed, pasture	lahi
殊	particularly, especially, exceptionally	espesyal
殖	augment, increase, multiply, raise	pagdaragdag

Kanji	Meaning	Translation
艦 (N1)	warship	pandigma
輩 (N1)	comrade, fellow, people, companions	kasama
穴 (N1)	hole, aperture, slit, cave, den	butas
奇 (N1)	strange, strangeness, curiosity	kakaiba
慢 (N1)	ridicule, laziness	panunuya
鶴 (N1)	crane, stork	kreyn
謀 (N1)	conspire, cheat, impose on, plan, devise, scheme	pagsasabwatan
暖 (N1)	warmth	init
昌 (N1)	prosperous, bright, clear	maunlad
拍 (N1)	clap, beat (music)	pumalakpak
朗 (N1)	melodious, clear, bright, serene, cheerful	malambing
寛 (N1)	tolerant, leniency, generosity, relax, feel at home	mapagparaya
覆 (N1)	capsize, cover, shade, mantle, be ruined	takip
胞 (N1)	placenta, sac, sheath	kaluban
泣 (N1)	cry, weep, moan	iyak
隔 (N1)	isolate, alternate, distance, separate, gulf	ibukod
浄 (N1)	clean, purify, cleanse, exorcise, Manchu Dynasty	malinis
没 (N1)	drown, sink, hide, fall into, disappear, die	nalunod
暇 (N1)	spare time, rest, leisure, time, leave of absence	paglilibang
肺 (N1)	lungs	baga

Kanji	Meaning	Translation
貞 (N1)	upright, chastity, constancy, righteousness	patayo
靖 (N1)	peaceful	mapayapa
鑑 (N1)	specimen, take warning from, learn from	ispesimen
飼 (N1)	domesticate, raise, keep, feed	mapagpayaman
陰 (N1)	shade, yin, negative, sex organs, secret, shadow	lilim
銘 (N1)	inscription, signature (of artisan)	inskripsyon
随 (N1)	follow, though, notwithstanding	Sundin
烈 (N1)	ardent, violent, vehement, furious, severe, extreme	masigasig
尋 (N1)	inquire, fathom, look for	magtanong
稿 (N1)	draft, copy, manuscript, straw	draft
丹 (N1)	rust-colored, red, red lead, pills	pula
啓 (N1)	disclose, open, say	ibunyag
也 (N1)	to be (classical)	at saka
丘 (N1)	hill, knoll	burol
壌 (N1)	lot, earth, soil	lupa
漫 (N1)	cartoon, involuntarily, in spite of oneself	cartoon
玄 (N1)	mysterious, occultness	misteryoso
粘 (N1)	sticky, glutinous, greasy, persevere	dumikit
悟 (N1)	enlightenment, perceive, discern, realize	paliwanag
舗 (N1)	shop, store	shop

Kanji	Meaning	Filipino
妊 (N1)	pregnancy	Pagbubuntis
熟 (N1)	mellow, ripen, mature, acquire skill	malambing
旭 (N1)	rising sun, morning sun	araw
恩 (N1)	grace, kindness, goodness, favor, mercy	kabaitan
騰 (N1)	inflation, advancing, going	inflation
往 (N1)	journey, chase away, let go, going, travel	paglalakbay
豆 (N1)	beans, pea, midget	beans
遂 (N1)	consummate, accomplish, attain, commit (suicide)	natapos
狂 (N1)	lunatic, insane, crazy, confuse	nakalulungkot
岐 (N1)	branch off, fork in road, scene, arena, theater	eksena
陛 (N1)	highness, steps (of throne)	mataas
緯 (N1)	horizontal, woof, left & right, latitude	pahalang
培 (N1)	cultivate, foster	linangin
衰 (N1)	decline, wane, weaken	tanggihan
艇 (N1)	rowboat, small boat	Bangka
屈 (N1)	yield, bend, flinch, submit	Bend
径 (N1)	diameter, path, method	landas
淡 (N1)	thin, faint, pale, fleeting	maputla
抽 (N1)	pluck, pull, extract, excel	pumutok
披 (N1)	expose, open	ilantad

Kanji	Meaning	Filipino
廷 (N1)	courts, imperial court, government office	mga korte
錦 (N1)	brocade, fine dress, honors	Brocade
准 (N1)	quasi-, semi-, associate	iugnay
暑 (N1)	sultry, hot, summer heat	init
磯 (N1)	seashore, beach	baybayin
奨 (N1)	exhort, urge, encourage	payo
浸 (N1)	immersed, soak, dip, steep, moisten, wet, dunk	nalubog
剰 (N1)	surplus, besides	labis
胆 (N1)	gall bladder, courage, pluck, nerve	lakas ng loob
繊 (N1)	slender, fine, thin kimono	payat
駒 (N1)	pony, horse, colt	Foal
虚 (N1)	void, emptiness, unpreparedness, crack, fissure	kawalan ng laman
霊 (N1)	spirits, soul	espiritu
帳 (N1)	notebook, account book, album	kuwaderno
悔 (N1)	repent, regret	panghihinayang
諭 (N1)	rebuke, admonish, charge, warn, persuade	saway
惨 (N1)	wretched, disaster, cruelty, harsh	kakila-kilabot
虐 (N1)	tyrannize, oppress	mapang-api
翻 (N1)	flip, turn over, wave, flutter, change (mind)	lumiko
墜 (N1)	crash, fall (down)	pagkahulog

Kanji	Meaning	Translation
沼 N1	marsh, lake, bog, swamp, pond	Marsh
据 N1	set, lay a foundation, install, equip, squat down	ayon kay
肥 N1	fertilizer, get fat, fertile, manure, pamper	pataba
徐 N1	gradually, slowly, deliberately, gently	unti-unti
糖 N1	sugar	asukal
搭 N1	board, load (a vehicle), ride	sumakay
盾 N1	shield, escutcheon, pretext	kalasag
脈 N1	vein, pulse, hope	pulso
滝 N1	waterfall, rapids, cascade	talon
軌 N1	rut, wheel, track, model, way of doing	rut
俵 N1	bag, bale, sack, counter for bags	bag
妨 N1	disturb, prevent, hamper, obstruct	mang-istorbo
擦 N1	grate, rub, scratch, scrape, chafe, scour	kuskusin
鯨 N1	whale	balyena
荘 N1	villa, inn, cottage, feudal manor	bahay-panuluyan
諾 N1	consent, assent, agreement	pahintulot
雷 N1	thunder, lightening bolt	kulog
漂 N1	drift, float (on liquid)	naaanod na
懐 N1	pocket, feelings, heart, yearn, miss someone	damdamin
勘 N1	intuition, perception	intuwisyon

Kanji	Meaning	Tagalog
栽 (N1)	plantation, planting	pagtatanim
拐 (N1)	kidnap, falsify	pagkidnap
駄 (N1)	burdensome, pack horse, horse load, send by horse	pabigat
添 (N1)	annexed, accompany, marry, suit, meet	samahan
冠 (N1)	crown, best, peerless	korona
斜 (N1)	diagonal, slanting, oblique	pahilis
鏡 (N1)	mirror, speculum, barrel-head	salamin
聡 (N1)	wise, fast learner	marunong
浪 (N1)	wandering, waves, billows	alon
亜 (N1)	Asia, rank next, come after, -ous	Asya
覧 (N1)	perusal, see	pagtanggi
詐 (N1)	lie, falsehood, deceive, pretend	kasinungalingan
壇 (N1)	podium, stage, rostrum, terrace	podium
勲 (N1)	meritorious deed, merit	merito
魔 (N1)	witch, demon, evil spirit	bruha
酬 (N1)	repay, reward, retribution	magbayad
紫 (N1)	purple, violet	lila
曙 (N1)	dawn, daybreak	Tanghali
紋 (N1)	family crest, figures	Pattern
卸 (N1)	wholesale	pakyawan

Kanji	Meaning	Tagalog
奮	stirred up, be invigorated, flourish	umunlad
欄	column, handrail, blank, space	haligi
逸	deviate, idleness, leisure, miss the mark, evade	lumihis
涯	horizon, shore	abot-tanaw
拓	clear (the land), open, break up (land)	Pagpapalawak
眼	eyeball	mata
獄	prison, jail	kulungan
尚	esteem, furthermore, still, yet	pagpapahalaga
彫	carve, engrave, chisel	kinatay
穏	calm, quiet, moderation	mahinahon
顕	appear, existing	lumitaw
巧	adroit, skilled, ingenuity	talino sa paglikha
矛	halberd, arms, festival float	halberd
垣	hedge, fence, wall	bakod
欺	deceit, cheat, delude	panlilinlang
萩	bush clover	bush klouber
粛	solemn, quietly, softly	solemne
栗	chestnut	kastanyas
愚	foolish, folly, absurdity, stupid	bobo
遭	encounter, meet, party, association, interview	nakatagpo

Kanji	Meaning	Translation
架 (N1)	erect, frame, mount, support, shelf, construct	frame
鬼 (N1)	ghost, devil	multo
庶 (N1)	commoner, all, bastard	pangkaraniwan
稚 (N1)	immature, young	Walang muwang
滋 (N1)	nourishing, more & more, be luxuriant	Masarap
幻 (N1)	phantasm, vision, dream, illusion, apparition	phantasm
煮 (N1)	boil, cook	lutuin
姫 (N1)	princess	prinsesa
誓 (N1)	vow, swear, pledge	sumumpa
把 (N1)	grasp, faggot, bunch, counter for bundles	hawakan
践 (N1)	tread, step on, trample, practice, carry through	Pagsasanay
呈 (N1)	display, offer, present, send, exhibit	pagpapakita
疎 (N1)	alienate, rough, neglect, shun, sparse	lumayo
仰 (N1)	face-up, look up, depend, seek, respect, rever	Hanapin
剛 (N1)	sturdy, strength	matatag
疾 (N1)	rapidly	mabilis
征 (N1)	subjugate, attack the rebellious, collect taxes	magpasakop
砕 (N1)	smash, break, crush, familiar, popular	mabasag
嫁 (N1)	marry into, bride	ikakasal
謙 (N1)	self-effacing, humble oneself, condescend	Mababang-loob

Kanji	Meaning	Tagalog
后	empress, queen, after, behind, back, later	impression
嘆	sigh, lament, moan, grieve	hininga
菌	germ, fungus, bacteria	bakterya
鎌	sickle, scythe, trick	karit
巣	nest, rookery, hive, cobweb, den	pugad
頻	repeatedly, recur	dalas
琴	harp, koto	alpa
班	squad, corps, unit, group	pulutong
棚	shelf, ledge, rack, mount, mantle, trellis	istante
潔	undefiled, pure, clean, righteous, gallant	walang dungis
酷	cruel, severe, atrocious, unjust	malupit
宰	superintend, manager, rule	superintendente
廊	corridor, hall, tower	koridor
寂	loneliness, quietly, mellow, mature	malungkot
辰	sign of the dragon, 7-9AM	Dragon
霞	be hazy, grow dim, blurred	malabo
伏	prostrated, bend down, bow, cover, lay (pipes)	nakayuko
碁	Go	Pumunta
俗	vulgar, customs, manners, worldliness	Vulgar
漠	vague, obscure, desert, wide	disyerto

Kanji	Meaning	Filipino
邪	wicked, injustice, wrong	kasamaan
晶	sparkle, clear, crystal	kristal
墨	black ink, India ink, ink stick, Mexico	tinta
鎮	tranquilize, ancient peace-preservation centers	tahimik
洞	den, cave, excavation	yungib
履	footgear, shoes, boots, put on (the feet	sapatos
劣	inferiority, be inferior to, be worse	mas mababa
那	what?	Ano?
殴	assault, hit, beat, thrash	pag-atake
娠	with child, pregnancy	buntis
奉	observance, offer, present, dedicate	pagmamasid
憂	melancholy, grieve, lament, be anxious, sad	mapanglaw
朴	crude, simple, plain, docile	bastos
亭	pavilion, restaurant, mansion, arbor, cottage	pavilion
淳	pure	puro
怪	suspicious, mystery, apparition	kahina-hinala
鳩	pigeon, dove	kalapati
酔	drunk, feel sick, poisoned, elated, spellbound	lasing
惜	pity, be sparing of, frugal, stingy, regret	Kawawa
穫	harvest, reap	ani

All entries: N1

Kanji	Meaning	Translation
佳 (N1)	excellent, beautiful, good, pleasing, skilled	mahusay
潤 (N1)	wet, be watered, profit by, receive benefits	Moisten
悼 (N1)	lament, grieve over	humagulgol
乏 (N1)	destitution, scarce, limited	kapalaran
該 (N1)	above-stated, the said, that specific	tiyak
赴 (N1)	proceed, get, become, tend	magpatuloy
桑 (N1)	mulberry	mulberi
桂 (N1)	Japanese Judas-tree, cinnamon tree	puno ng kanela
髄 (N1)	marrow, pith	Marmol
虎 (N1)	tiger, drunkard	tigre
盆 (N1)	basin, lantern festival, tray	palanggana
晋 (N1)	advance	advance
穂 (N1)	ear, ear (grain), head, crest (wave)	tainga
壮 (N1)	robust, manhood, prosperity	malakas
堤 (N1)	dike, bank, embankment	dike
飢 (N1)	hungry, starve	gutom
傍 (N1)	bystander, side, besides, while, nearby, 3rd person	bystander
疫 (N1)	epidemic	epidemya
累 (N1)	accumulate, involvement, trouble, tie up	makaipon
痴 (N1)	stupid, foolish	Idiot

搬 N1 conveyor, carry, transport lumipat	**晃** N1 clear malinaw	**癒** N1 healing, cure, quench (thirst), wreak paglunas	**寸** N1 measurement, foot, 10 pagsukat
郭 N1 enclosure, quarters, fortification enclosure	**尿** N1 urine ihi	**凶** N1 villain, evil, bad luck, disaster kontrabida	**吐** N1 spit, vomit, belch, confess, tell (lies) dumura
宴 N1 banquet, feast, party piging	**鷹** N1 hawk agila	**賓** N1 V.I.P., guest bisita	**虜** N1 captive, barbarian, low epithet for the enemy bihag
陶 N1 pottery, porcelain palayok	**鐘** N1 bell, gong, chimes kampana	**憾** N1 remorse, regret, be sorry panghihinayang	**猪** N1 boar baboy
紘 N1 large malaki	**磁** N1 magnet, porcelain magnetic	**弥** N1 all the more, increasingly lalong dumarami	**昆** N1 descendants, elder brother, insect inapo

Kanji	Meaning	Filipino
粗 (N1)	coarse, rough, rugged	magaspang
訂 (N1)	revise, correct, decide	baguhin
芽 (N1)	bud, sprout, spear, germ	usbong
庄 (N1)	level	antas
傘 (N1)	umbrella	payong
敦 (N1)	industry, kindliness	industriya
騎 (N1)	equestrian, riding on horses	pantay-pantay
寧 (N1)	rather, preferably	sa halip
循 (N1)	sequential, fellow	sunud-sunod
忍 (N1)	endure, bear, put up with, conceal, secrete	magtiis
怠 (N1)	neglect, laziness	pagpapabaya
如 (N1)	likeness, like, such as, as if, better, best, equal	pagkakahawig
寮 (N1)	dormitory, hostel, villa, tea pavillion	dormitoryo
祐 (N1)	help	tumulong
鵬 (N1)	phoenix	phoenix
鉛 (N1)	lead	humantong
珠 (N1)	pearl, gem, jewel	perlas
苗 (N1)	seedling, sapling, shoot	punla
獣 (N1)	animal, beast	hayop
哀 (N1)	pathetic, grief, sorrow, pathos, pity, sympathize	kalunus-lunos

Kanji	Meaning	Filipino
跳 (N1)	hop, leap up, spring, jerk, prance, buck, splash	tumalon
匠 (N1)	artisan, workman, carpenter	artisan
垂 (N1)	droop, suspend, hang, slouch	tumulo
蛇 (N1)	snake, serpent, hard drinker	ahas
澄 (N1)	lucidity, be clear, clear, clarify, settle, strain	Malinaw
縫 (N1)	sew, stitch, embroider	tahiin
僧 (N1)	Buddhist priest, monk	monghe
眺 (N1)	stare, watch, look at, see, scrutinize	tumitig
亘 (N1)	span, request	span
呉 (N1)	give, do something for	magbigay
凡 (N1)	mediocre	katamtaman
憩 (N1)	recess, rest, relax, repose	pag-urong
媛 (N1)	beautiful woman, princess	prinsesa
溝 (N1)	gutter, ditch, sewer, drain, 10**32	talampas
恭 (N1)	respect, reverent	paggalang
刈 (N1)	reap, cut, clip, trim, prune	umani
睡 (N1)	drowsy, sleep, die	antok
錯 (N1)	confused, mix, be in disorder	nalilito
伯 (N1)	chief, count, earl, uncle, Brazil	hepe
笹 (N1)	bamboo grass	damo ng kawayan

Kanji	Meaning	Filipino
穀 (N1)	cereals, grain	butil
陵 (N1)	mausoleum, imperial tomb	mausoleum
霧 (N1)	fog, mist	ulap
魂 (N1)	soul, spirit	kaluluwa
弊 (N1)	abuse, evil, vice, breakage	pang-aabuso
妃 (N1)	queen, princess	reyna
舶 (N1)	liner, ship	barko
餓 (N1)	starve, hungry, thirst	gutom
窮 (N1)	hard up, destitute, suffer, perplexed, cornered	magdusa
掌 (N1)	manipulate, rule, administer, conduct, palm of hand	pagmamanipula
麗 (N1)	lovely, companion	kaibig-ibig
綾 (N1)	design, figured cloth, twill	disenyo
臭 (N1)	stinking, ill-smelling, suspicious looking	mabango
悦 (N1)	ecstasy, joy, rapture	Natutuwa
刃 (N1)	blade, sword, edge	talim
縛 (N1)	truss, arrest, bind, tie, restrain	truss
暦 (N1)	calendar, almanac	kalendaryo
宜 (N1)	best regards, good	pinakamahusay na pagbati
盲 (N1)	blind, blind man, ignoramus	bulag
粋 (N1)	chic, style, purity, essence, pith, cream, elite	chic

Kanji	Meaning	Filipino
辱	embarrass, humiliate, shame	nakakahiya
毅	strong	malakas
轄	control, wedge	kontrol
猿	monkey	unggoy
弦	bowstring, chord, hypotenuse	bowstring
稔	harvest, ripen	Pag-aani
窒	plug up, obstruct	hadlangan
炊	cook, boil	Nagluluto
洪	deluge, flood, vast	delubyo
摂	vicarious, surrogate, act in addition to	kapalit
飽	sated, tired of, bored, satiate	pagod
冗	superfluous, uselessness	mababaw
桃	peach tree	Peach
狩	hunt, raid, gather	pangangaso
朱	vermilion, cinnabar, scarlet, red, bloody	vermilion
渦	whirlpool, eddy, vortex	eddy
紳	sire, good belt, gentleman	ginoo
枢	hinge, pivot, door	bisagra
碑	tombstone, monument	bantayog
鍛	forge, discipline, train	Forge

刀 — sword, saber, knife — tabak (N1)	**鼓** — drum, beat, rouse, muster — tambol (N1)	**裸** — naked, nude, uncovered, partially clothed — hubo't hubad (N1)	**猶** — furthermore, still, yet — at saka (N1)
塊 — clod, lump, chink, clot, mass — clod (N1)	**旋** — rotation, go around — pag-ikot (N1)	**弓** — bow, bow (archery, violin) — yumuko (N1)	**幣** — cash, bad habit, humble prefix, gift — cash (N1)
膜 — membrane — lamad (N1)	**扇** — fan, folding fan — tagahanga (N1)	**腸** — intestines, guts, bowels, viscera — bituka (N1)	**槽** — vat, tub, tank — vat (N1)
慈 — mercy — awa (N1)	**楊** — willow — willow (N1)	**伐** — fell, strike, attack, punish — nahulog (N1)	**駿** — a good horse, speed, a fast person — bilis (N1)
糾 — twist, ask, investigate, verify — iuwi sa ibang bagay (N1)	**亮** — clear, help — maliwanag (N1)	**墳** — tomb, mound — libingan (N1)	**坪** — two-mat area, ~36 sq ft — Ping (N1)

Kanji	Meaning	Filipino
紺	dark blue, navy	asul
娯	recreation, pleasure	libangan
舌	tongue, reed, clapper	dila
羅	gauze, thin silk, Rome	gasa
峡	gorge, ravine	gorge
俸	stipend, salary	Salary
厘	rin, 1, 10sen, 1, 10bu	Sentro
峰	summit, peak	tugatog
圭	square jewel, corner, angle, edge	sulok
醸	brew, cause	magluto
蓮	lotus	lotus
弔	condolences, mourning, funeral	condolences
乙	the latter, duplicate, strange, witty	Kopyahin
汁	soup, juice, broth, sap, gravy, pus	katas
尼	nun	madre
遍	everywhere, times, widely, generally	kahit saan
衡	equilibrium, measuring rod, scale	punto ng balanse
薫	send forth fragrance, fragrant, be scented	mabango
猟	game-hunting, shooting, game, bag	pagbaril
羊	sheep	tupa

Kanji	Meaning	Filipino
款 (N1)	goodwill, article, section, friendship, collusion	mabuting kalooban
閲 (N1)	review, inspection, revision	pagsusuri
偵 (N1)	spy	spy
喝 (N1)	hoarse, scold	mabaho
敢 (N1)	daring, sad, tragic, pitiful, frail, feeble	mangahas
胎 (N1)	womb, uterus	sinapupunan
酵 (N1)	fermentation	lebadura
豚 (N1)	pork, pig	baboy
遮 (N1)	intercept, interrupt, obstruct	pangharang
扉 (N1)	front door, title page, front page	pambungad na pintuan
硫 (N1)	sulphur	asupre
赦 (N1)	pardon, forgiveness	kapatawaran
窃 (N1)	stealth, steal, secret, private, hushed	magnakaw
泡 (N1)	bubbles, foam, suds, froth	bubble
瑞 (N1)	congratulations	pagbati
又 (N1)	or again, furthermore, on the other hand	at saka
慨 (N1)	rue, be sad, sigh, lament	mapagbigay
紡 (N1)	spinning	Umiikot
恨 (N1)	regret, bear a grudge, resentment, malice, hatred	panghihinayang
肪 (N1)	obese, fat	napakataba

Kanji	Meaning	Tagalog
扶 (N1)	aid, help, assist	tumulong
戯 (N1)	frolic, play, sport	frolic
伍 (N1)	5, 5-man squad, file, line	linya
忌 (N1)	mourning, abhor, detestable, death anniversary	pagdadalamhati
濁 (N1)	voiced, uncleanness, wrong, nigori, impurity	karumihan
奔 (N1)	bustle, run	Tumakbo
斗 (N1)	Big Dipper, 10 sho (vol), sake dipper	Balde
蘭 (N1)	orchid, Holland	orchid
迅 (N1)	swift, fast	mabilis
肖 (N1)	resemblance	pagkakahawig
鉢 (N1)	bowl, rice tub, pot, crown	Bowl
朽 (N1)	decay, rot, remain in seclusion	bulok
殻 (N1)	husk, nut shell	husk
享 (N1)	receive, undergo, answer (phone), take, get, catch	sumailalim
秦 (N1)	Manchu dynasty	Dinastiya ng Manchu
茅 (N1)	miscanthus reed	miscanthus tambo
藩 (N1)	clan, enclosure	enclosure
沙 (N1)	sand	buhangin
輔 (N1)	help	pantulong
媒 (N1)	mediator, go-between	tagapamagitan

Kanji	Meaning	Filipino
鶏	chicken	manok
禅	Zen, silent meditation	pagmumuni-muni
嘱	entrust, request, send a message	ipagkatiwala
胴	trunk, torso, hull (ship), hub of wheel	Torso
迭	transfer, alternation	paglipat
挿	insert, put in, graft, wear (sword)	Ipasok
嵐	storm, tempest	bagyo
椎	oak, mallet	oak
絹	silk	Sutla
陪	obeisance, follow, accompany, attend on	yumuko
剖	divide	hatiin
譜	musical score, music, note, staff, table, genealogy	musika
郁	cultural progress, perfume	pabango
悠	permanence, distant, long time, leisure	pagkapanatili
淑	graceful, gentle, pure	maganda
帆	sail	maglayag
暁	daybreak, dawn, in the event	madaling araw
傑	greatness, excellence	kadakilaan
楠	camphor tree	puno ng camphor
笛	flute, clarinet, pipe, whistle, bagpipe, piccolo	plauta

Kanji	Meaning	Filipino
玲	sound of jewels	mga hiyas
奴	guy, slave, manservant, fellow	alipin
錠	lock, fetters, shackles	kandado
拳	fist	kamao
遷	transition, move, change	lumipat
拙	bungling, clumsy, unskillful	pangit
侍	waiter, samurai, wait upon, serve	Weyter
尺	shaku, Japanese foot, measure, scale, rule	sukatin
峠	mountain peak, mountain pass, climax	kasukdulan
篤	fervent, kind, cordial, serious, deliberate	marubdob
肇	beginning	simula
渇	thirst, dry up, parch	nauuhaw
叔	uncle, youth	tiyuhin
雌	feminine, female	babae
亨	undergo, answer (phone), take, get, catch	sumailalim
堪	withstand, endure, support, resist	Worthy
叙	confer, relate, narrate, describe	ibigay
酢	vinegar, sour, acid, tart	suka
吟	versify, singing, recital	magpakilala
遞	relay, in turn, sending	relay

All entries marked N1.

Kanji	Meaning	Translation
嶺 (N1)	peak, summit	summit
甚 (N1)	tremendously, very, great, exceedingly	napaka
喬 (N1)	high, boasting	ipinagmamalaki
崇 (N1)	adore, respect, revere, worship	pagsamba
漆 (N1)	lacquer, varnish, seven	pintura
岬 (N1)	headland, cape, spit, promontory	kapa
癖 (N1)	mannerism, habit, vice, trait, fault, kink	paraan
愉 (N1)	pleasure, happy, rejoice	Masaya
寅 (N1)	sign of the tiger, 3-5AM	tigre
礁 (N1)	reef, sunken rock	bahura
乃 (N1)	from, possessive particle, whereupon, accordingly	mula sa
洲 (N1)	continent, sandbar, island, country	Kontinente
屯 (N1)	barracks, police station, camp	kuwartel
樺 (N1)	birch	birch
槙 (N1)	twig, ornamental evergreen	twig
姻 (N1)	matrimony, marry	matrimonya
巌 (N1)	rock, crag, boulder	bato
擬 (N1)	mimic, aim (a gun) at, nominate, imitate	gayahin
塀 (N1)	fence, wall, (kokuji)	bakod
唇 (N1)	lips	labi

睦 — intimate, friendly, harmonious — intimate	閑 — leisure — paglilibang	胡 — barbarian, foreign — barbarian	幽 — seclude, confine to a room — liblib
峻 — high, steep — mataas	曹 — cadet, friend — kadete	詠 — recitation, poem, song, composing — pagtula	卑 — lowly, base, vile, vulgar — mababa
侮 — scorn, despise, make light of, contempt — pangungutya	鋳 — casting, mint — paghahagis	抹 — rub, paint, erase — punasan	尉 — military officer, jailer, old man, rank — Kapitan
隷 — slave, servant, prisoner, criminal, follower — alipin	禍 — calamity, misfortune, evil, curse — kapahamakan	蝶 — butterfly — paruparo	酪 — dairy products, whey, broth, fruit juice — whey
茎 — stalk, stem — tangkay	帥 — commander, leading troops, governor — kumandante	逝 — departed, die — Namatay	汽 — vapor, steam — singaw

Kanji	Meaning	Translation
琢 (N1)	polish	polish
匿 (N1)	hide, shelter, shield	tago
襟 (N1)	collar, neck, lapel	kwelyo
蛍 (N1)	lightning-bug, firefly	sunog
蕉 (N1)	banana	saging
寡 (N1)	widow, minority, few	Balo
琉 (N1)	lapis lazuli	lapis Lazuli
痢 (N1)	diarrhea	pagtatae
庸 (N1)	commonplace, ordinary, employment	pangkaraniwan
朋 (N1)	companion, friend	Kaibigan
坑 (N1)	pit, hole	hukay
藍 (N1)	indigo	asul
賊 (N1)	burglar, rebel, traitor, robber	magnanakaw
搾 (N1)	squeeze	Kalat
畔 (N1)	paddy ridge, levee	levee
遼 (N1)	distant	malayong
唄 (N1)	songs with samisen	umawit
孔 (N1)	cavity, hole, slit, very, great, exceedingly	butas
橘 (N1)	mandarin orange	Tangerine
漱 (N1)	gargle, rinse mouth	banlawan

Kanji	Meaning	Filipino
呂	spine, backbone	gulugod
拷	torture, beat	pahirap
嬢	lass, girl, Miss, daughter	babae
苑	garden, farm, park	hardin
巽	southeast	silangan
杜	woods, grove	gubat
渓	mountain stream, valley	lambak
翁	venerable old man	matandang lalaki
廉	bargain, reason, charge, suspicion	bargain
謹	discreet, reverently, humbly	mahinahon
瞳	pupil	mag-aaral
湧	boil, ferment, seethe, uproar, breed	pakuluan
欣	take pleasure in, rejoice	magalak
窯	kiln, oven, furnace	kilig
褒	praise, extol	papuri
醜	ugly, unclean, shame, bad looking	pangit
升	measuring box, 1.8 liter	kahon ng pagsukat
煩	anxiety, trouble, worry, pain, ill, annoy	pagkabalisa
巴	comma-design	koma
禎	happiness	kaligayahan

Kanji	Meaning	Tagalog
劾	censure, criminal investigation	pagsisiyasat
堕	degenerate, descend to, lapse into	lumala
租	tariff, crop tax, borrowing	upa
稜	angle, edge, corner, power, majesty	gilid
桟	scaffold, cleat, frame, jetty, bolt (door)	plantsa
倭	Yamato, ancient Japan	Hapon
婿	bridegroom, son-in-law	ikakasal
斐	beautiful, patterned	maganda
罷	quit, stop, leave, withdraw, go	tumigil
矯	rectify, straighten, correct, reform, cure	Tama
某	so-and-so, one, a certain, that person	tiyak
囚	captured, criminal, arrest, catch	Mga Bilanggo
魁	charging ahead of others	singilin
虹	rainbow	bahaghari
鴻	large bird, wild goose	gansa
泌	ooze, flow, soak in, penetrate, secrete	Secrete
於	at, in, on, as for	sa
赳	strong and brave	matapang
漸	steadily, gradually advancing, finally, barely	unti-unti
蚊	mosquito	lamok

Kanji	Meaning (EN)	Meaning (TL)
葵	hollyhock	hollyhock
厄	unlucky, misfortune, bad luck, disaster	walang imik
藻	seaweed, duckweed	damong-dagat
禄	fief, allowance, pension, grant, happiness	allowance
孟	chief, beginning	simula
嫡	legitimate wife, direct descent (non-bastard)	Unang asawa
尭	high, far	mataas
嚇	menacing, dignity, majesty, threaten	dangal
凸	convex, beetle brow, uneven	Convex
暢	stretch	mag-inat
韻	rhyme, elegance, tone	tula
霜	frost	Frost
硝	nitrate, saltpeter	Nitrate
勅	imperial order	Order ng imperyal
芹	parsley	perehil
杏	apricot	aprikot
棺	coffin, casket	kabaong
儒	Confucian	Confucianism
鳳	male mythical bird	phoenix
馨	fragrant, balmy, favourable	mabango

Kanji	Meaning	Tagalog
慧	wise	marunong
愁	distress, grieve, lament, be anxious	pagkabalisa
楼	watchtower, lookout, high building	relo
彬	refined, gentle	banayad
匡	correct, save, assist	tama
眉	eyebrow	kilay
欽	respect, revere, long for	paggalang
薪	fuel, firewood, kindling	gasolina
褐	brown, woollen kimono	kayumanggi
賜	grant, gift, boon, results	magbigay
嵯	steep, craggy, rugged	matarik
綜	rule	panuntunan
繕	darning, repair, mend, trim, tidy up, adjust	darning
栓	plug, bolt, cork, bung, stopper	plug
翠	green	berde
鮎	freshwater trout, smelt	Pito
榛	hazelnut, filbert	mapanganib
凹	concave, hollow, sunken	malukot
艶	glossy, luster, glaze, polish, charm, colorful	makintab
惣	all	lahat

Kanji	Meaning	Filipino
蔦 (N1)	vine, ivy	puno ng ubas
錬 (N1)	tempering, refine, drill, train, polish	nakakainis
隼 (N1)	falcon	Falcon
渚 (N1)	strand, beach, shore	baybayin
衷 (N1)	inmost, heart, mind, inside	pusod
逐 (N1)	pursue, drive away, chase, accomplish, attain	habulin
斥 (N1)	reject, retreat, recede, withdraw, repel, repulse	tanggihan
稀 (N1)	rare, phenomenal, dilute (acid)	dilute
芙 (N1)	lotus, Mt Fuji	lotus
皋 (N1)	swamp, shore	swamp
雛 (N1)	chick, squab, duckling, doll	Manok
惟 (N1)	consider, reflect, think	isaalang-alang
佑 (N1)	help, assist	tumulong
耀 (N1)	shine, sparkle, gleam, twinkle	Shine
黛 (N1)	blackened eyebrows	kilay
渥 (N1)	kindness	kabaitan
憧 (N1)	yearn after, long for, aspire to, admire, adore	humanga
宵 (N1)	wee hours, evening, early night	gabi
妄 (N1)	delusion, unnecessarily, without authority	maling akala
惇 (N1)	sincere, kind, considerate	taos-puso

Kanji	Meaning	Tagalog
脩	dried meat	pinatuyong karne
甫	for the first time, not until	lang
酌	bar-tending, serving sake, the host, draw (water)	ladle
蚕	silkworm	silkworm
嬉	glad, pleased, rejoice	magalak
蒼	blue, pale	maputla
暉	shine, light	lumiwanag
頒	distribute, disseminate, partition, understand	ipamahagi
只	only, free, in addition	lamang
肢	limb, arms & legs	paa
檀	cedar, sandlewood, spindle tree	sedro
凱	victory song	awit ng tagumpay
彗	comet	Kometa
嗣	heir, succeed	Tagapagmana
叶	grant, answer	sagot
汐	eventide, tide, salt water, opportunity	Pag-ulan
絢	kimono design	Napakarilag
朔	conjunction (astronomy), first day of month	magkakasama
伽	nursing, attending, entertainer	pag-aalaga
畝	furrow, 30 tsubo, ridge, rib	tudling

Kanji	Meaning	Tagalog
抄	extract, selection, summary, copy, spread thin	kopya
爽	refreshing, bracing, resonant, sweet, clear	nakakapreskong
黎	dark, black, many	madilim
惰	lazy, laziness	Malas ang loob
蛮	barbarian	barbarian
冴	be clear, serene, cold, skilful	matahimik
旺	flourishing, successful, beautiful, vigorous	umunlad
萌	show symptoms of, sprout, bud, malt	umusbong
偲	recollect, remember	paggunita
壱	I, one	isa
瑠	lapis lazuli	lapis Lazuli
允	license, sincerity, permit	lisensya
蒔	sow (seeds)	buto
鯉	carp	carp
弧	arc, arch, bow	arko
遥	far off, distant, long ago	liblib
瑛	sparkle of jewelry, crystal	kristal
附	affixed, attach, refer to, append	Maglakip
彪	spotted, mottled, patterned, small tiger	namintal
但	however, but	ngunit

綺 N1 figured cloth, beautiful maganda	**芋** N1 potato patatas	**茜** N1 madder, red dye, Turkey red madder	**凌** N1 endure, keep (rain)out, stave off, tide over magtiis
皓 N1 white, clear maputi	**洸** N1 sparkling water Sparkling tubig	**毬** N1 burr, ball burr	**婆** N1 old woman, grandma, wet nurse lola
緋 N1 scarlet, cardinal iskarlata	**鯛** N1 sea bream, red snapper Sea bream	**怜** N1 wise marunong	**邑** N1 village, rural community nayon
傲 N1 emulate, imitate Tularan	**碧** N1 blue, green berde	**啄** N1 peck, pick up peck	**穰** N1 good crops, prosperity pananim
酉 N1 west, bird, sign of the bird kanluran	**倹** N1 frugal, economy, thrifty matipid	**柚** N1 citron citron	**繭** N1 cocoon cocoon

亦 N1 also, again din	**詢** N1 consult with kumonsulta	**采** N1 dice, form, appearance, take, coloring dais	**紗** N1 gauze, gossamer gasa
賦 N1 levy, ode, prose, poem, tribute, installment pagpapauwi	**眸** N1 pupil of the eye mata	**玖** N1 beautiful black jewel, nine siyam	**弍** N1 two, second dalawa
錘 N1 weight, plumb bob, sinker bigat	**諄** N1 tedious nakakapagod	**倖** N1 happiness, luck sa kabutihang-palad	**痘** N1 pox, smallpox bulutong
笙 N1 a reed instrument tambo	**侃** N1 strong, just, righteous, peace-loving malakas	**裟** N1 Buddhist surplice surplice	**洵** N1 alike, truth Tunay
爾 N1 you, thou, second person ikaw	**耗** N1 decrease bumaba	**昴** N1 the Pleiades Mga Pleiades	**銑** N1 pig iron Paggiling

Kanji	Meaning	Translation
莞 (N1)	reed used to cover tatami	tambo
伶 (N1)	actor	aktor
碩 (N1)	large, great, eminent	malaki
宥 (N1)	soothe, calm, pacify	kumalma
滉 (N1)	deep and broad	malalim
晏 (N1)	late, quiet, sets (sun)	huli na
伎 (N1)	deed, skill	kasanayan
朕 (N1)	majestic plural, imperial we	Ako
迪 (N1)	edify, way, path	landas
綸 (N1)	thread, silk cloth	sinulid
且 (N1)	moreover, also, furthermore	bukod dito
竣 (N1)	end, finish	Kumpleto
晨 (N1)	morning, early	umaga
吏 (N1)	officer, an official	Opisyal
燦 (N1)	brilliant	napakatalino
麿 (N1)	I, you, (kokuji)	Ako
頌 (N1)	eulogy	eulogy
箇 (N1)	counters for things	mga counter
楓 (N1)	maple	maple
琳 (N1)	jewel, tinkling of jewelry	hiyas

梧 N1 Chinese parasol tree, phoenix tree punong phoenix	**哉** N1 how, what, alas, (question mark) paano	**澪** N1 water route, shipping channel channel	**晟** N1 clear malinaw
衿 N1 neck, collar, lapel leeg	**凪** N1 lull, calm, (kokuji) mahinahon	**梢** N1 treetops, twig twig	**丙** N1 third class, 3rd, 3rd calendar sign pangatlo
颯 N1 suddenly, smoothly maayos	**茄** N1 eggplant talong	**勺** N1 ladle, one tenth of a go, dip ladle	**恕** N1 excuse, tolerate, forgive pasensya
瑚 N1 ancestral offering receptacle koral	**遵** N1 abide by, follow, obey, learn Sundin	**瞭** N1 clear malinaw	**燎** N1 burn, bonfire paso
虞 N1 uneasiness, fear, anxiety, concern takot	**柊** N1 holly holly	**侑** N1 urge to eat kumain	**謁** N1 audience, audience (with king) madla

Kanji	Meaning	Translation
斤 (N1)	axe, 1.32 lb, catty, counter for loaves of bread	palakol
嵩 (N1)	be aggravated, grow worse, grow bulky, swell	namamaga
捺 (N1)	press, print, affix a seal, stamp	Pindutin pababa
蓉 (N1)	lotus	lotus
茉 (N1)	jasmine	jasmine
燿 (N1)	shine	Shine
誼 (N1)	friendship, intimacy	pagkakaibigan
冶 (N1)	melting, smelting	Ngumiti
栞 (N1)	bookmark, guidebook	bookmark
墾 (N1)	ground-breaking, open up farmland	Paglinang
勁 (N1)	strong	lakas
菖 (N1)	iris	iris
椋 (N1)	type of deciduous tree, grey starling	Mga Starlings
叡 (N1)	intelligence, imperial	katalinuhan
胤 (N1)	descendent, issue, offspring	inapo
凜 (N1)	cold, strict, severe	malamig
亥 (N1)	sign of the hog, 9-11PM	hog
爵 (N1)	baron, peerage, court rank	baron
脹 (N1)	dilate, distend, bulge, fill out, swell	dilate
麟 (N1)	Chinese unicorn, genius, giraffe, bright, shining	henyo

莉 N1 jasmine jasmine	**汰** N1 luxury, select luho	**瑶** N1 beautiful as a jewel hiyas	**瑳** N1 polish polish
耶 N1 question mark tandang pananong	**椰** N1 coconut tree Coconut	**絃** N1 string, cord, samisen music string	**丞** N1 help tumulong
璃 N1 glassy, lapis lazuli Salamin	**奎** N1 star, god of literature bituin	**塑** N1 model, molding Mould	**昂** N1 rise tumaas
柾 N1 straight grain, spindle tree, (kokuji) butil	**熙** N1 bright, sunny, prosperous, merry maliwanag	**菫** N1 the violet lila	**諒** N1 fact, reality, understand, appreciate maintindihan
鞠 N1 ball bola	**崚** N1 towering in a row paghatak	**濫** N1 excessive, overflow, spread out sobra	**捷** N1 victory, fast Mabilis

Printed in Japan
落丁、乱丁本のお問い合わせは
Amazon.co.jp カスタマーサービスへ